JULIUS K. NYERERE

# Ujamaa-

# Essays

# on

# Socialism

## OXFORD UNIVERSITY PRESS

*London   Oxford   New York*

OXFORD UNIVERSITY PRESS

Oxford    London    Glasgow
New York    Toronto    Melbourne    Wellington
Nairobi    Dar es Salaam    Cape Town
Kuala Lumpur    Singapore    Jakarta    Hong Kong    Tokyo
Delhi    Bombay    Calcutta    Madras    Karachi

First published by
Oxford University Press, Dar es Salaam, 1968

First published as
an Oxford University Press paperback, 1968

This reprint, 1979

*Printed in the United States of America*

*Ujamaa—Essays on Socialism* is the English version of President J. K. Nyerere's Swahili book *Ujamaa.*

# Contents

# Preface

TANU has been officially committed to the building of a socialist society since early 1962, but for a long time the meaning of this philosophy in the conditions of Tanzania was left vague. The pamphlet 'Ujamaa', published in 1962, described the basic attitudes of socialism, but it was published in English and was never easily available to the people of Tanzania. Many active party workers, and also many of our teachers and civil servants, therefore remained unclear about even the most important principles of the socialism they were responsible for promoting or serving.

This lack of an ideology did not prevent the Government and Party from pursuing policies which were in fact socialist; nor did it affect the commitment of TANU and the post-independence Governments to the service of the masses of the people. The conversion of all freehold land into leasehold ownership on the grounds that land must belong to the people as a whole, the public purchase of the private electricity service company, and the increasing emphasis on public ownership or participation in the economic development activities, were all socialist actions taken deliberately. So too was the encouragement of marketing co-operatives, the introduction of protective labour legislation and minimum wage increases, and the gradual change in the system of taxation so that the burden of supporting public expenditure fell more heavily on those with higher income. In addition, the introduction of a more appropriate form of political democracy emphasized the sovereignty of the people—which is a basic tenet of socialism.

Despite these and many other socialist measures, however, it gradually became clear that the absence of a generally accepted and easily understood statement of philosophy and policy was allowing some Government and Party actions which were not consistent with the building of socialism, and which even encouraged the growth of non-socialist values and attitudes. Thus, for example, the Africanization for which TANU had campaigned during the independence struggle was being interpreted to mean the replacement of non-African landlords, employers, and capitalists by African ones. Also, the increasing number of Africans driving large cars or living in luxurious houses was being advanced as a sign of national progress. Meanwhile the masses of the people were continuing to live in poverty, because their conditions of life were not affected by such transfer of privilege from non-citizens to citizens.

The Arusha Declaration, adopted by TANU in February 1967, supplied the need for a definition of socialism in Tanzanian terms, and provided the necessary sign-post of the direction in which the nation must travel to achieve its goals. Throughout the succeeding year, further statements and speeches elaborated on the policy implications of the Arusha Declaration, and explained more about the relationship between this socialist philosophy and other doctrines of life and society.

The primary purpose of this book is to make this material available in a convenient form for use by the leaders and educators of the new Tanzania. Its secondary purpose is to contribute to the growth of a wider international understanding of the aspirations and purposes of the Tanzanian people, and perhaps to promote further discussion about the relevance and requirements of socialism in relation to mankind's march to the future.

*July 1968*                                        *J. K. Nyerere*

# 1

# Ujamaa-
# The Basis of African
# Socialism

*Published as a TANU pamphlet in April 1962*

Socialism—like democracy—is an attitude of mind. In a socialist society it is the socialist attitude of mind, and not the rigid adherence to a standard political pattern, which is needed to ensure that the people care for each other's welfare.

The purpose of this paper is to examine that attitude. It is not intended to define the institutions which may be required to embody it in a modern society.

In the individual, as in the society, it is an attitude of mind which distinguishes the socialist from the non-socialist. It has nothing to do with the possession or non-possession of wealth. Destitute people can be potential capitalists— exploiters of their fellow human beings. A millionaire can equally well be a socialist; he may value his wealth only because it can be used in the service of his fellow men. But the man who uses wealth for the purpose of dominating any of his fellows is a capitalist. So is the man who would if he could!

I have said that a millionaire can be a good socialist. But a socialist millionaire is a rare phenomenon. Indeed he is almost a contradiction in terms. The appearance of millionaires in any society is no proof of its affluence;

they can be produced by very poor countries like Tanganyika just as well as by rich countries like the United States of
America. For it is not efficiency of production, nor the
amount of wealth in a country, which make millionaires; it
is the uneven distribution of what is produced. The basic
difference between a socialist society and a capitalist society
does not lie in their methods of producing wealth, but in the
way that wealth is distributed. While, therefore, a millionaire could be a good socialist, he could hardly be the
product of a socialist society.

Since the appearance of millionaires in a society does
not depend on its affluence, sociologists may find it interest-
ing to try and find out why our societies in Africa did not,
in fact, produce any millionaires—for we certainly had
enough wealth to create a few. I think they would discover
that it was because the organization of traditional African
society—its distribution of the wealth it produced—was
such that there was hardly any room for parasitism. They
might also say, of course, that as a result of this Africa
could not produce a leisured class of landowners, and therefore there was nobody to produce the works of art or
science which capitalist societies can boast. But works of
art and the achievements of science are products of the
intellect—which, like land, is one of God's gifts to man.
And I cannot believe that God is so careless as to have made
the use of one of His gifts depend on the *misuse* of another!

Defenders of capitalism claim that the millionaire's
wealth is the just reward for his ability or enterprise.
But this claim is not borne out by the facts. The wealth
of the millionaire depends as little on the enterprise or
abilities of the millionaire himself as the power of a feudal
monarch depended on his own efforts, enterprise or brain.
Both are users, exploiters, of the abilities and enterprise
of other people. Even when you have an exceptionally

intelligent and hard-working millionaire, the difference between his intelligence, his enterprise, his hard work, and those of other members of society, cannot possibly be proportionate to the difference between their 'rewards'. There must be something wrong in a society where one man, however hard-working or clever he may be, can acquire as great a 'reward' as a thousand of his fellows can acquire between them.

Acquisitiveness for the purpose of gaining power and prestige is unsocialist. In an acquisitive society wealth tends to corrupt those who possess it. It tends to breed in them a desire to live more comfortably than their fellows, to dress better, and in every way to outdo them. They begin to feel they must climb as far above their neighbours as they can. The visible contrast between their own comfort and the comparative discomfort of the rest of society becomes almost essential to the enjoyment of their wealth, and this sets off the spiral of personal competition—which is then anti-social.

Apart from the anti-social effects of the accumulation of personal wealth, the very desire to accumulate it must be interpreted as a vote of 'no confidence' in the social system. For when a society is so organized that it cares about its individuals, then, provided he is willing to work, no individual within that society should worry about what will happen to him tomorrow if he does not hoard wealth today. Society itself should look after him, or his widow, or his orphans. This is exactly what traditional African society succeeded in doing. Both the 'rich' and the 'poor' individual were completely secure in African society. Natural catastrophe brought famine, but it brought famine to everybody—'poor' or 'rich'. Nobody starved, either of food or of human dignity, because he lacked personal wealth; he could depend on the wealth possessed by the community of which he was a member. That was socialism. That *is* socialism. There can be no such thing as acquisitive socialism, for that would be another contradiction in terms. Socialism is essentially distributive. Its concern is to see that those who sow reap a fair share of what they sow.

The production of wealth, whether by primitive or modern methods, requires three things. First, land. God has given us the land, and it is from the land that we get the raw materials which we reshape to meet our needs. Secondly, tools. We have found by simple experience that tools do help! So we make the hoe, the axe, or the modern factory or tractor, to help us to produce wealth—the goods we need. And, thirdly, human exertion—or labour. We don't need to read Karl Marx or Adam Smith to find out that neither the land nor the hoe actually produces wealth. And we don't need to take degrees in Economics to know that neither the worker nor the landlord produces land. Land is God's gift to man—it is always there. But we do know, still without degrees in Economics, that the axe and the plough were produced by the labourer. Some of our more sophisticated friends apparently have to undergo the most rigorous intellectual training simply in order to discover that stone axes were produced by that ancient gentleman 'Early Man' to make it easier for him to skin the impala he had just killed with a club, which he had also made for himself!

In traditional African society *everybody* was a worker. There was no other way of earning a living for the community. Even the Elder, who appeared to be enjoying himself without doing any work and for whom everybody else appeared to be working, had, in fact, worked hard all his younger days. The wealth he now appeared to possess was not *his*, personally; it was only 'his' as the Elder of the group which had produced it. He was its guardian. The wealth itself gave him neither power nor prestige. The respect paid to him by the young was his because he was older than they, and had served his community longer; and the 'poor' Elder enjoyed as much respect in our society as the 'rich' Elder.

When I say that in traditional African society everybody was a worker, I do not use the word 'worker' simply as opposed to 'employer' but also as opposed to 'loiterer' or 'idler'. One of the most socialistic achievements of our society was the sense of security it gave to its members, and the universal hospitality on which they could rely. But it is too often forgotten, nowadays, that the basis of this great socialistic achievement was this: that it was taken for granted that every member of society—barring only the children and the infirm—contributed his fair share of effort towards the production of its wealth. Not only was the capitalist, or the landed exploiter, unknown to traditional African society, but we did not have that other form of modern parasite—the loiterer, or idler, who accepts the hospitality of society as his 'right' but gives nothing in return! Capitalistic exploitation was impossible. Loitering was an unthinkable disgrace.

Those of us who talk about the African way of life and, quite rightly, take a pride in maintaining the tradition of hospitality which is so great a part of it, might do well to remember the Swahili saying: '*Mgeni siku mbili; siku ya tatu mpe jembe*'—or in English, 'Treat your guest as a guest for two days; on the third day give him a hoe!' In actual fact, the guest was likely to ask for the hoe even before his host had to give him one—for he knew what was expected of him, and would have been ashamed to remain idle any longer. Thus, working was part and parcel, was indeed the very basis and justification of this socialist achievement of which we are so justly proud.

There is no such thing as socialism without work. A society which fails to give its individuals the means to work, or, having given them the means to work, prevents them from getting a fair share of the products of their own sweat and toil, needs putting right. Similarly, an individual who can work—and is provided by society with the means to work—but does not do so, is equally wrong. He has no right to expect anything from society because he contributes nothing to society.

The other use of the word 'worker', in its specialized sense of 'employee' as opposed to 'employer', reflects a capitalist attitude of mind which was introduced into Africa with the coming of colonialism and is totally foreign to our own way of thinking. In the old days the African had never aspired to the possession of personal wealth for the purpose of dominating any of his fellows. He had never had labourers or 'factory hands' to do his work for him. But then came the—foreign capitalists. They were wealthy. They were powerful. And the African naturally started wanting to be wealthy too. There is nothing wrong in our wanting to be wealthy; nor is it a bad thing for us to want to acquire the power which wealth brings with it. But it most certainly is wrong if we want the wealth and the power so that we can dominate somebody else. Unfortunately there are some of us who have already learnt to covet wealth for that purpose—and who would like to use the methods which the capitalist uses in acquiring it. That is to say, some of us would like to use, or exploit, our brothers for the purpose of building up our own personal power and prestige. This is completely foreign to us, and it is incompatible with the socialist society we want to build here.

Our first step, therefore, must be to re-educate ourselves; to regain our former attitude of mind. In our traditional African society we were individuals within a community.

We took care of the community, and the community took care of us. We neither needed nor wished to exploit our fellow men.

And in rejecting the capitalist attitude of mind which colonialism brought into Africa, we must reject also the capitalist methods which go with it. One of these is the individual ownership of land. To us in Africa land was always recognized as belonging to the community. Each individual within our society had a right to the use of land, because otherwise he could not earn his living and one cannot have the right to life without also having the right to some means of maintaining life. But the African's right to land was simply the right to use it; he had no other right to it, nor did it occur to him to try and claim one.

The foreigner introduced a completely different concept —the concept of land as a marketable commodity. According to this system, a person could claim a piece of land as his own private property whether he intended to use it or not. I could take a few square miles of land, call them 'mine', and then go off to the moon. All I had to do to gain a living from 'my' land was to charge a rent to the people who wanted to use it. If this piece of land was in an urban area I had no need to develop it at all; I could leave it to the fools who were prepared to develop all the other pieces of land surrounding 'my' piece, and in doing so automatically to raise the market value of mine. Then I could come down from the moon and demand that these fools pay me through their noses for the high value of 'my' land—a value which they themselves had created for me while I was enjoying myself on the moon! Such a system is not only foreign to us, it is completely wrong. Landlords, in a society which recognizes individual ownership of land, can be, and usually are, in the same class as the loiterers I was talking about: the class of parasites.

We must not allow the growth of parasites here in Tanganyika. The TANU Government must go back to the traditional African custom of land-holding. That is to say a member of society will be entitled to a piece of land *on condition that he uses it*. Unconditional, or 'freehold', ownership of land (which leads to speculation and parasitism) must be abolished. We must, as I have said, regain our former attitude of mind—our traditional African socialism—and apply it to the new societies we are building today. TANU has pledged itself to make socialism the basis of its policy in every field. The people of Tanganyika have given us their mandate to carry out that policy, by electing a TANU Government to lead them. So the Government can be relied upon to introduce only legislation which is in harmony with socialist principles.

But, as I said at the beginning, true socialism is an attitude of mind. It is therefore up to the people of Tanganyika —the peasants, the wage-earners, the students, the leaders, all of us—to make sure that this socialist attitude of mind is not lost through the temptations to personal gain (or to the abuse of positions of authority) which may come our way as individuals, or through the temptation to look on the good of the whole community as of secondary importance to the interests of our own particular group.

Just as the Elder, in our former society, was respected for his age and his service to the community, so, in our modern society, this respect for age and service will be preserved. And in the same way as the 'rich' Elder's apparent wealth was really only held by him in trust for his people, so, today, the apparent extra wealth which certain positions of leadership may bring to the individuals who fill them, can be theirs only in so far as it is a necessary aid to the carrying out of their duties. It is a 'tool' entrusted to them for the benefit of the people they serve. It is not 'theirs' personally; and they may not use any part of it as a means of accumulating more for their own benefit, nor as an 'insurance' against the day when they no longer hold the same positions. That would be to betray the people who entrusted it to them. If they serve the community while they can, the community must look after them when they are no longer able to do so.

In tribal society, the individuals or the families within a tribe were 'rich' or 'poor' according to whether the whole tribe was rich or poor. If the tribe prospered all the members of the tribe shared in its prosperity. Tanganyika, today, is a poor country. The standard of living of the masses of our people is shamefully low. But if every man and woman in the country takes up the challenge and works to the limit of his or her ability for the good of the whole society, Tanganyika will prosper; and that prosperity will be shared by all her people.

But it must be shared. The true socialist may not exploit his fellows. So that if the members of any group within our society are going to argue that, because they happen to be contributing more to the national income than some other groups, they must therefore take for themselves a greater share of the profits of their own industry than they actually need; and if they insist on this in spite of the fact that it would mean reducing their group's contribution to the general income and thus slowing down the rate at which the whole community can benefit, then that group is exploiting (or trying to exploit) its fellow human beings. It is displaying a capitalist attitude of mind.

There are bound to be certain groups which, by virtue of the 'market value' of their particular industry's products, will contribute more to the nation's income than others. But the others may actually be producing goods or services which are of equal, or greater, intrinsic value although they do not happen to command such a high artificial value. For example, the food produced by the peasant farmer is of greater social value than the diamonds mined at Mwadui. But the mine-workers of Mwadui could claim, quite correctly, that their labour was yielding greater financial profits to the community than that of the farmers. If, however, they went on to demand that they should therefore be given most of that extra profit for themselves, and that no share of it should be spent on helping the farmers, they would be potential capitalists!

This is exactly where the attitude of mind comes in. It is one of the purposes of trade unions to ensure for the workers a fair share of the profits of their labour. But a 'fair' share must be fair in relation to the whole society. If it is greater than the country can afford without having to penalize some other section of society, then it is not a fair share. Trade union leaders and their followers, as long as they are true socialists, will not need to be coerced by the Government into keeping their demands within the limits imposed by the needs of society as a whole. Only if there are potential capitalists amongst them will the socialist government have to step in and prevent them from putting their capitalist ideas into practice!

As with groups, so with individuals. There are certain skills, certain qualifications, which, for good reasons, command a higher rate of salary for their possessors than others. But, here again, the true socialist will demand only that return for his skilled work which he knows to be a fair one in proportion to the wealth or poverty of the whole society to which he belongs. He will not, unless he is a would-be capitalist, attempt to blackmail the community by demanding a salary equal to that paid to his counterpart in some far wealthier society.

European socialism was born of the Agrarian Revolution and the Industrial Revolution which followed it. The former created the 'landed' and the 'landless' classes in society; the latter produced the modern capitalist and the industrial proletariat.

These two revolutions planted the seeds of conflict within society, and not only was European socialism born of that conflict, but its apostles sanctified the conflict itself into a philosophy. Civil war was no longer looked upon as something evil, or something unfortunate, but as something good and necessary. As prayer is to Christianity or to Islam, so civil war (which they call 'class war') is to the European version of socialism—a means inseparable from the end. Each becomes the basis of a whole way of life. The European socialist cannot think of his socialism without its father—capitalism!

Brought up in tribal socialism, I must say I find this contradiction quite intolerable. It gives capitalism a philosophical status which capitalism neither claims nor deserves. For it virtually says, 'Without capitalism, and the conflict which capitalism creates within society, there can be no socialism'! This glorification of capitalism by the doctrinaire European socialists, I repeat, I find intolerable.

African socialism, on the other hand, did not have the 'benefit' of the Agrarian Revolution or the Industrial Revolution. It did not start from the existence of conflicting 'classes' in society. Indeed I doubt if the equivalent for the word 'class' exists in any indigenous African language; for language describes the ideas of those who speak it, and the idea of 'class' or 'caste' was non-existent in African society.

The foundation, and the objective, of African socialism is the extended family. The true African socialist does not look on one class of men as his brethren and another as his natural enemies. He does not form an alliance with the 'brethren' for the extermination of the 'non-brethren'.

He rather regards *all* men as his brethren—as members of his ever extending family. That is why the first article of TANU's Creed is: '*Binadamu wote ni ndugu zangu, na Afrika ni moja*'. If this had been originally put in English, it could have been: 'I believe in Human Brotherhood and the Unity of Africa'.

'Ujamaa', then, or 'Familyhood', describes our socialism. It is opposed to capitalism, which seeks to build a happy society on the basis of the exploitation of man by man; and it is equally opposed to doctrinaire socialism which seeks to build its happy society on a philosophy of inevitable conflict between man and man.

We, in Africa, have no more need of being 'converted' to socialism than we have of being 'taught' democracy. Both are rooted in our own past—in the traditional society which produced us. Modern African socialism can draw from its traditional heritage the recognition of 'society' as an extension of the basic family unit. But it can no longer confine the idea of the social family within the limits of the tribe, nor, indeed, of the nation. For no true African socialist can look at a line drawn on a map and say, 'The people on this side of that line are my brothers, but those who happen to live on the other side of it can have no claim on me'; every individual on this continent is his brother.

It was in the struggle to break the grip of colonialism that we learnt the need for unity. We came to recognize that the same socialist attitude of mind which, in the tribal days, gave to every individual the security that comes of belonging to a widely extended family, must be preserved within the still wider society of the nation. But we should not stop there. Our recognition of the family to which we all belong must be extended yet further—beyond the tribe, the community, the nation, or even the continent—to embrace the whole society of mankind. This is the only logical conclusion for true socialism.

# 2

# The Arusha Declaration

## 5 February 1967

*The Declaration was discussed and then published in Swahili. This revised English translation clarifies ambiguities which existed in the translation originally issued.*

---

### THE ARUSHA DECLARATION
### AND TANU'S POLICY ON SOCIALISM
### AND SELF-RELIANCE

### PART ONE

### The TANU Creed

The policy of TANU is to build a socialist state. The principles of socialism are laid down in the TANU Constitution and they are as follows:

WHEREAS TANU believes:

(a)  That all human beings are equal;

(b)  That every individual has a right to dignity and respect;

(c)  That every citizen is an integral part of the nation and has the right to take an equal part in Government at local, regional and national level;

(d)  That every citizen has the right to freedom of expression, of movement, of religious belief and of association within the context of the law;

(e)  That every individual has the right to receive from society protection of his life and of property held according to law;

(f) That every individual has the right to receive a just return for his labour;

(g) That all citizens together possess all the natural re-sources of the country in trust for their descendants;

(h) That in order to ensure economic justice the state must have effective control over the principal means of production; and

(i) That it is the responsibility of the state to intervene actively in the economic life of the nation so as to ensure the well-being of all citizens, and so as to prevent the exploitation of one person by another or one group by another, and so as to prevent the accumulation of wealth to an extent which is inconsistent with the existence of a classless society.

NOW, THEREFORE, the principal aims and objects of TANU shall be as follows:

(a) To consolidate and maintain the independence of this country and the freedom of its people;

(b) To safeguard the inherent dignity of the individual in accordance with the Universal Declaration of Human Rights;

(c) To ensure that this country shall be governed by a democratic socialist government of the people;

(d) To co-operate with all political parties in Africa engaged in the liberation of all Africa;

(e) To see that the Government mobilizes all the resources of this country towards the elimination of poverty, ignorance and disease;

(f) To see that the Government actively assists in the formation and maintenance of co-operative organizations;

(g) To see that wherever possible the Government itself directly participates in the economic development of this country;

(h) To see that the Government gives equal opportunity to all men and women irrespective of race, religion or status;

(i) To see that the Government eradicates all types of exploitation, intimidation, discrimination, bribery and corruption;

(j) To see that the Government exercises effective control over the principal means of production and pursues policies which facilitate the way to collective ownership of the resources of this country;

(k) To see that the Government co-operates with other states in Africa in bringing about African unity;

(l) To see that Government works tirelessly towards world peace and security through the United Nations Organization.

## PART TWO

### The Policy of Socialism

(a) *Absence of Exploitation*

A truly socialist state is one in which all people are workers and in which neither capitalism nor feudalism exists. It does not have two classes of people, a lower class composed of people who work for their living, and an upper class of people who live on the work of others. In a really socialist country no person exploits another; everyone who is physically able to work does so; every worker obtains a just return for the labour he performs; and the incomes derived from different types of work are not grossly divergent.

In a socialist country, the only people who live on the work of others, and who have the right to be dependent

upon their fellows, are small children, people who are too
old to support themselves, the crippled, and those whom
the state at any one time cannot provide with an opportunity
to work for their living.

Tanzania is a nation of peasants and workers, but it is
not yet a socialist society. It still contains elements of
feudalism and capitalism—-with their temptations. These
feudalistic and capitalistic features of our society could
spread and entrench themselves.

(b) *The Major Means of Production and Exchange are
    under the Control of the Peasants and Workers*

To build and maintain socialism it is essential that all
the major means of production and exchange in the nation
are controlled and owned by the peasants through the
machinery of their Government and their co-operatives.
Further, it is essential that the ruling Party should be a
Party of peasants and workers.

The major means of production and exchange are such
things as: land; forests; minerals; water; oil and electricity;
news media; communications; banks, insurance, import
and export trade, wholesale trade; iron and steel, machine-
tool, arms, motor-car, cement, fertilizer, and textile industries; and any big factory on which a large section of the
people depend for their living, or which provides essential
components of other industries; large plantations, and
especially those which provide raw materials essential to
important industries.

Some of the instruments of production and exchange
which have been listed here are already owned or controlled
by the people's Government of Tanzania.

(c) *The Existence of Democracy*

A state is not socialist simply because its means of

production and exchange are controlled or owned by the government, either wholly or in large part. For a country to be socialist, it is essential that its government is chosen and led by the peasants and workers themselves. If the minority governments of Rhodesia or South Africa controlled or owned the entire economies of these respective countries, the result would be a strengthening of oppression, not the building of socialism. True socialism cannot exist without democracy also existing in the society.

### (d) *Socialism is a Belief*

Socialism is a way of life, and a socialist society cannot simply come into existence. A socialist society can only be built by those who believe in, and who themselves practise, the principles of socialism. A committed member of TANU will be a socialist, and his fellow socialists—that is, his fellow believers in this political and economic system—are all those in Africa or elsewhere in the world who fight for the rights of peasants and workers. The first duty of a TANU member, and especially of a TANU leader, is to accept these socialist principles, and to live his own life in accordance with them. In particular, a genuine TANU leader will not live off the sweat of another man, nor commit any feudalistic or capitalistic actions.

The successful implementation of socialist objectives depends very much upon the leaders, because socialism is a belief in a particular system of living, and it is difficult for leaders to promote its growth if they do not themselves accept it.

## PART THREE

### The Policy of Self-Reliance

*We are at War*

TANU is involved in a war against poverty and oppres-

sion in our country; the struggle is aimed at moving the
people of Tanzania (and the people of Africa as a whole)
from a state of poverty to a state of prosperity.

We have been oppressed a great deal, we have been
exploited a great deal and we have been disregarded a great
deal. It is our weakness that has led to our being oppressed,
exploited and disregarded. Now we want a revolution—
a revolution which brings to an end our weakness, so that
we are never again exploited, oppressed, or humiliated.

## *A Poor Man does not use Money as a Weapon*

But it is obvious that in the past we have chosen the
wrong weapon for our struggle, because we chose money as
our weapon. We are trying to overcome our economic
weakness by using the weapons of the economically strong—
weapons which in fact we do not possess. By our thoughts,
words and actions it appears as if we have come to the
conclusion that without money we cannot bring about
the revolution we are aiming at. It is as if we have said,
'Money is the basis of development. Without money there
can be no development.'

That is what we believe at present. TANU leaders,
and Government leaders and officials, all put great emphasis
and dependence on money. The people's leaders, and the
people themselves, in TANU, NUTA, Parliament, UWT,
the co-operatives, TAPA, and in other national institutions
think, hope and pray for MONEY. It is as if we had all
agreed to speak with one voice, saying, 'If we get money we
shall develop, without money we cannot develop'.

In brief, our Five-Year Development Plan aims at more
food, more education, and better health; but the weapon
we have put emphasis upon is money. It is as if we said,
'In the next five years we want to have more food, more
education, and better health, and in order to achieve these

things we shall spend £250,000,000'. We think and speak as if the most important thing to depend upon is MONEY and anything else we intend to use in our struggle is of minor importance.

When a Member of Parliament says that there is a shortage of water in his constituency and he asks the Government how it intends to deal with the problem, he expects the Government to reply that it is planning to remove the shortage of water in his constituency—WITH MONEY.

When another Member of Parliament asks what the Government is doing about the shortage of roads, schools or hospitals in his constituency, he also expects the Government to tell him that it has specific plans to build roads, schools and hospitals in his constituency—WITH MONEY.

When a NUTA official asks the Government about its plans to deal with the low wages and poor housing of the workers, he expects the Government to inform him that the minimum wage will be increased and that better houses will be provided for the workers—WITH MONEY.

When a TAPA official asks the Government what plans it has to give assistance to the many TAPA schools which do not get Government aid, he expects the Government to state that it is ready the following morning to give the required assistance—WITH MONEY.

When an official of the co-operative movement mentions any problem facing the farmer, he expects to hear that the Government will solve the farmer's problems—WITH MONEY. In short, for every problem facing our nation, the solution that is in everybody's mind is MONEY.

Each year, each Ministry of Government makes its estimates of expenditure, i.e. the amount of money it will require in the coming year to meet recurrent and development expenses. Only one Minister and his Ministry make estimates of revenue. This is the Minister for Finance.

Every Ministry puts forward very good development plans. When the Ministry presents its estimates, it believes that the money is there for the asking but that the Minister for Finance and his Ministry are being obstructive. And regularly each year the Minister for Finance has to tell his fellow Ministers that there is no money. And each year the Ministries complain about the Ministry of Finance when it trims down their estimates.

Similarly, when Members of Parliament and other leaders demand that the Government should carry out a certain development, they believe that there is a lot of money to spend on such projects, but that the Government is the stumbling block. Yet such belief on the part of Ministries, Members of Parliament and other leaders does not alter the stark truth, which is that Government has no money.

When it is said that Government has no money, what does this mean? It means that the people of Tanzania have insufficient money. The people pay taxes out of the very little wealth they have; it is from these taxes that the Government meets its recurrent and development expenditure. When we call on the Government to spend more money on development projects, we are asking the Government to use more money. And if the Government does not have any more, the only way it can do this is to increase its revenue through extra taxation.

If one calls on the Government to spend more, one is in effect calling on the Government to increase taxes. Calling on the Government to spend more without raising taxes is like demanding that the Government should perform miracles; it is equivalent to asking for more milk from a cow while insisting that the cow should not be milked again. But our refusal to admit that calling on the Government to spend more is the same as calling on the Government to raise taxes shows that we fully realize the difficulties of increasing taxes. We realize that the cow has no more milk—that is, that the people find it difficult to pay more taxes. We know that the cow would like to have more milk herself, so that her calves could drink it, or that she would like more milk which could be sold to provide more comfort for herself or her calves. But knowing all the things which could be done with more milk does not alter the fact that the cow has no more milk!

## WHAT OF EXTERNAL AID?

One method we use to try and avoid a recognition of the need to increase taxes if we want to have more money for development, is to think in terms of getting the extra money from outside Tanzania. Such external finance falls into three main categories.

(a) *Gifts:* This means that another government gives our Government a sum of money as a free gift for a particular development scheme. Sometimes it may be that an institution in another country gives our Government, or an institution in our country, financial help for development programmes.

(b) *Loans:* The greater portion of financial help we expect to get from outside is not in the form of gifts or charity, but in the form of loans. A foreign government or a foreign institution, such as a bank, lends our Government money for the purposes of development. Such a loan has repayment conditions attached to it, covering such factors as the time period for which it is available and the rate of interest.

(c) *Private Investment:* The third category of financial help is also greater than the first. This takes the form of investment in our country by individuals or companies from outside. The important condition which such private investors have in mind is that the enterprise into

which they put their money should bring them profit and
that our Government should permit them to repatriate
these profits. They also prefer to invest in a country
whose policies they agree with and which will safeguard
their economic interests.

These three are the main categories of external finance.
And there is in Tanzania a fantastic amount of talk about
getting money from outside. Our Government, and different
groups of our leaders, never stop thinking about methods
of getting finance from abroad. And if we get some money
or even if we just get a promise of it, our newspapers, our
radio, and our leaders, all advertise the fact in order that
every person shall know that salvation is coming, or is on
the way. If we receive a gift we announce it, if we receive
a loan we announce it, if we get a new factory we announce
it—and always loudly. In the same way, when we get a
promise of a gift, a loan, or a new industry, we make an
announcement of the promise. Even when we have merely
started discussions with a foreign government or institution
for a gift, a loan, or a new industry, we make an announcement—even though we do not know the outcome of the
discussions. Why do we do all this? Because we want people
to know that we have started discussions which will bring
prosperity.

DO NOT LET US DEPEND UPON MONEY FOR DEVELOPMENT

It is stupid to rely on money as the major instrument of
development when we know only too well that our country
is poor. It is equally stupid, indeed it is even more stupid,
for us to imagine that we shall rid ourselves of our poverty
through foreign financial assistance rather than our own
financial resources. It is stupid for two reasons.

Firstly, we shall not get the money. It is true that there are
countries which can, and which would like to, help us.

But there is no country in the world which is prepared to give us gifts or loans, or establish industries, to the extent that we would be able to achieve all our development targets. There are many needy countries in the world. And even if all the prosperous nations were willing to help the needy countries, the assistance would still not suffice. But in any case the prosperous nations have not accepted a responsibility to fight world poverty. Even within their own borders poverty still exists, and the rich individuals do not willingly give money to the government to help their poor fellow citizens.

It is only through taxation, which people have to pay whether they want to or not, that money can be extracted from the rich in order to help the masses. Even then there would not be enough money. However heavily we taxed the citizens of Tanzania and the aliens living here, the resulting revenue would not be enough to meet the costs of the development we want. And there is no World Government which can tax the prosperous nations in order to help the poor nations; nor if one did exist could it raise enough revenue to do all that is needed in the world. But in fact, such a World Government does not exist. Such money as the rich nations offer to the poor nations is given voluntarily, either through their own goodness, or for their own benefit. All this means that it is impossible for Tanzania to obtain from overseas enough money to develop our economy.

GIFTS AND LOANS WILL ENDANGER OUR INDEPENDENCE

Secondly, even if it were possible for us to get enough money for our needs from external sources, is this what we really want? Independence means self-reliance. Independence cannot be real if a nation depends upon gifts and loans from another for its development. Even if there was a nation, or nations, prepared to give us all the money we

need for our development, it would be improper for us to
accept such assistance without asking ourselves how this
would affect our independence and our very survival as a
nation. Gifts which increase, or act as a catalyst, to our
own efforts are valuable. But gifts which could have the
effect of weakening or distorting our own efforts should not
be accepted until we have asked ourselves a number of
questions.

The same applies to loans. It is true that loans are better
than 'free' gifts. A loan is intended to increase our efforts
or make those efforts more fruitful. One condition of a loan
is that you show how you are going to repay it. This means
you have to show that you intend to use the loan profitably
and will therefore be able to repay it.

But even loans have their limitations. You have to give
consideration to the ability to repay. When we borrow
money from other countries it is the Tanzanian who pays it
back. And as we have already stated, Tanzanians are
poor people. To burden the people with big loans, the repayment of which will be beyond their means, is not to
help them but to make them suffer. It is even worse when
the loans they are asked to repay have not benefited the
majority of the people but have only benefited a small
minority.

How about the enterprises of foreign investors? It is
true we need these enterprises. We have even passed an
Act of Parliament protecting foreign investments in this
country. Our aim is to make foreign investors feel that
Tanzania is a good place in which to invest because investments would be safe and profitable, and the profits can be
taken out of the country without difficulty. We expect to
get money through this method. But we cannot get enough.
And even if we were able to convince foreign investors
and foreign firms to undertake all the projects and pro-

grammes of economic development that we need, is that what we actually want to happen?

Had we been able to attract investors from America and Europe to come and start all the industries and all the projects of economic development that we need in this country, could we do so without questioning ourselves? Could we agree to leave the economy of our country in the hands of foreigners who would take the profits back to their countries? Or supposing they did not insist upon taking their profits away, but decided to reinvest them in Tanzania; could we really accept this situation without asking ourselves what disadvantages our nation would suffer? Would this allow the socialism we have said it is our objective to build?

How can we depend upon gifts, loans, and investments from foreign countries and foreign companies without endangering our independence? The English people have a proverb which says, 'He who pays the piper calls the tune'. How can we depend upon foreign governments and companies for the major part of our development without giving to those governments and countries a great part of our freedom to act as we please? The truth is that we cannot.

Let us repeat. We made a mistake in choosing money—something we do not have—to be the big instrument of our development. We are making a mistake to think that we shall get the money from other countries; first, because in fact we shall not be able to get sufficient money for our economic development; and secondly, because even if we could get all that we need, such dependence upon others would endanger our independence and our ability to choose our own political policies.

### WE HAVE PUT TOO MUCH EMPHASIS ON INDUSTRIES

Because of our emphasis on money, we have made another

big mistake. We have put too much emphasis on industries. Just as we have said, 'Without money there can be no development', we also seem to say, 'Industries are the basis of development, without industries there is no development'. This is true. The day when we have lots of money we shall be able to say we are a developed country. We shall be able to say, 'When we began our development plans we did not have enough money and this situation made it difficult for us to develop as fast as we wanted. Today we are developed and we have enough money'. That is to say, our money has been brought by development. Similarly, the day we become industrialized, we shall be able to say we are developed. Development would have enabled us to have industries. The mistake we are making is to think that development begins with industries. It is a mistake because we do not have the means to establish many modern industries in our country. We do not have either the necessary finances or the technical know-how. It is not enough to say that we shall borrow the finances and the technicians from other countries to come and start the industries. The answer to this is the same one we gave earlier, that we cannot get enough money and borrow enough technicians to start all the industries we need. And even if we could get the necessary assistance, dependence on it could interfere with our policy on socialism. The policy of inviting a chain of capitalists to come and establish industries in our country might succeed in giving us all the industries we need, but it would also succeed in preventing the establishment of socialism unless we believe that without first building capitalism, we cannot build socialism.

### LET US PAY HEED TO THE PEASANT
Our emphasis on money and industries has made us concentrate on urban development. We recognize that we

do not have enough money to bring the kind of development to each village which would benefit everybody. We also know that we cannot establish an industry in each village and through this means effect a rise in the real incomes of the people. For these reasons we spend most of our money in the urban areas and our industries are established in the towns.

Yet the greater part of this money that we spend in the towns comes from loans. Whether it is used to build schools, hospitals, houses or factories, etc., it still has to be repaid. But it is obvious that it cannot be repaid just out of money obtained from urban and industrial development. To repay the loans we have to use foreign currency which is obtained from the sale of our exports. But we do not now sell our industrial products in foreign markets, and indeed it is likely to be a long time before our industries produce for export. The main aim of our new industries is 'import substitution'—that is, to produce things which up to now we have had to import from foreign countries.

It is therefore obvious that the foreign currency we shall use to pay back the loans used in the development of the urban areas will not come from the towns or the industries. Where, then, shall we get it from? We shall get it from the villages and from agriculture. What does this mean? It means that the people who benefit directly from development which is brought about by borrowed money are not the ones who will repay the loans. The largest proportion of the loans will be spent in, or for, the urban areas, but the largest proportion of the repayment will be made through the efforts of the farmers.

This fact should always be borne in mind, for there are various forms of exploitation. We must not forget that people who live in towns can possibly become the exploiters of those who live in the rural areas. All our big hospitals are in towns and they benefit only a small section of the people of Tanzania. Yet if we have built them with loans from outside Tanzania, it is the overseas sale of the peasants' produce which provides the foreign exchange for repayment. Those who do not get the benefit of the hospitals thus carry the major responsibility for paying for them. Tarmac roads, too, are mostly found in towns and are of especial value to the motor-car owners. Yet if we have built those roads with loans, it is again the farmer who produces the goods which will pay for them. What is more, the foreign exchange with which the car was bought also came from the sale of the farmers' produce. Again, electric lights, water pipes, hotels and other aspects of modern development are mostly found in towns. Most of them have been built with loans, and most of them do not benefit the farmer directly, although they will be paid for by the foreign exchange earned by the sale of his produce. We should always bear this in mind.

Although when we talk of exploitation we usually think of capitalists, we should not forget that there are many fish in the sea. They eat each other. The large ones eat the small ones, and small ones eat those who are even smaller. There are two possible ways of dividing the people in our country. We can put the capitalists and feudalists on one side, and the farmers and workers on the other. But we can also divide the people into urban dwellers on one side and those who live in the rural areas on the other. If we are not careful we might get to the position where the real exploitation in Tanzania is that of the town dwellers exploiting the peasants.

### THE PEOPLE AND AGRICULTURE

The development of a country is brought about by people, not by money. Money, and the wealth it represents, is the result and not the basis of development. The four prerequisites of development are different; they are (i) People; (ii) Land; (iii) Good Policies; (iv) Good Leadership. Our country has more than ten million people* and its area is more than 362,000 square miles.

### AGRICULTURE IS THE BASIS OF DEVELOPMENT

A great part of Tanzania's land is fertile and gets sufficient rain. Our country can produce various crops for home consumption and for export.

We can produce food crops (which can be exported if we produce in large quantities) such as maize, rice, wheat, beans, groundnuts, etc. And we can produce such cash crops as sisal, cotton, coffee, tobacco, pyrethrum, tea, etc. Our land is also good for grazing cattle, goats, sheep, and for raising chickens, etc.; we can get plenty of fish from our rivers, lakes, and from the sea. All of our farmers are in areas which can produce two or three or even more of the food and cash crops enumerated above, and each farmer could increase his production so as to get more food or more money. And because the main aim of development is to get more food, and more money for our other needs, our purpose must be to increase production of these agricultural crops. This is in fact the only road through which we can develop our country—in other words, only by increasing our production of these things can we get more food and more money for every Tanzanian.

### THE CONDITIONS OF DEVELOPMENT

(a) *Hard Work*

Everybody wants development; but not everybody

---

* 1967 census showed 12.3 million people.

understands and accepts the basic requirements for development. The biggest requirement is hard work. Let us go to the villages and talk to our people and see whether or not it is possible for them to work harder.

In towns, for example, wage-earners normally work for seven and a half or eight hours a day, and for six or six and a half days a week. This is about 45 hours a week for the whole year, except for two or three weeks leave. In other words, a wage-earner works for 45 hours a week for 48 or 50 weeks of the year.

For a country like ours these are really quite short working hours. In other countries, even those which are more developed than we are, people work for more than 45 hours a week. It is not normal for a young country to start with such a short working week. The normal thing is to begin with long working hours and decrease them as the country becomes more and more prosperous. By starting with such short working hours and asking for even shorter hours, we are in fact imitating the more developed countries. And we shall regret this imitation. Nevertheless, wage-earners do work for 45 hours per week and their annual vacation does not exceed four weeks.

It would be appropriate to ask our farmers, especially the men, how many hours a week and how many weeks a year they work. Many do not even work for half as many hours as the wage-earner does. The truth is that in the villages the women work very hard. At times they work for 12 or 14 hours a day. They even work on Sundays and public holidays. Women who live in the villages work harder than anybody else in Tanzania. But the men who live in villages (and some of the women in towns) are on leave for half of their life. The energies of the millions of men in the villages and thousands of women in the towns which are at present wasted in gossip, dancing and drinking, are a great treasure which could contribute more towards the development of our country than anything we could get from rich nations.

We would be doing something very beneficial to our country if we went to the villages and told our people that they hold this treasure and that it is up to them to use it for their own benefit and the benefit of our whole nation.

## (b) *Intelligence*

The second condition of development is the use of intelligence. Unintelligent hard work would not bring the same good results as the two combined. Using a big hoe instead of a small one; using a plough pulled by oxen instead of an ordinary hoe; the use of fertilizers; the use of insecticides; knowing the right crop for a particular season or soil; choosing good seeds for planting; knowing the right time for planting, weeding, etc.; all these things show the use of knowledge and intelligence. And all of them combine with hard work to produce more and better results.

The money and time we spend on passing on this knowledge to the peasants are better spent and bring more benefits to our country than the money and great amount of time we spend on other things which we call development.

These facts are well known to all of us. The parts of our Five-Year Development Plan which are on target, or where the target has been exceeded, are those parts which depend solely upon the people's own hard work. The production of cotton, coffee, cashew nuts, tobacco and pyrethrum has increased enormously for the past three years. But these are things which are produced by hard work and the good leadership of the people, not by the use of great amounts of money.

Furthermore the people, through their own hard work and with a little help and leadership, have finished many

development projects in the villages. They have built
schools, dispensaries, community centres, and roads; they
have dug wells, water channels, animal dips, small dams,
and completed various other development projects. Had
they waited for money, they would not now have the use of
these things.

### HARD WORK IS THE ROOT OF DEVELOPMENT

Some Plan projects which depend on money are going on
well, but there are many which have stopped and others
which might never be fulfilled because of lack of money.
Yet still we talk about money and our search for money
increases and takes nearly all our energies. We should not
lessen our efforts to get the money we really need, but it
would be more appropriate for us to spend time in the
villages showing the people how to bring about development through their own efforts rather than going on so
many long and expensive journeys abroad in search of
development money. This is the real way to bring development to everybody in the country.

None of this means that from now on we will not need
money or that we will not start industries or embark upon
development projects which require money. Furthermore,
we are not saying that we will not accept, or even that we
shall not look for, money from other countries for our
development. This is *not* what we are saying. We will
continue to use money; and each year we will use more
money for the various development projects than we used
the previous year because this will be one of the signs
of our development.

What we are saying, however, is that from now on we
shall know what is the foundation and what is the fruit of
development. Between *money* and *people* it is obvious that
the people and their *hard work* are the foundation of develop-

ment, and money is one of the fruits of that hard work.

From now on we shall stand upright and walk forward on our feet rather than look at this problem upside down. Industries will come and money will come but their foundation is *the people* and their *hard work*, especially in AGRICULTURE. This is the meaning of self-reliance.

Our emphasis should therefore be on:
(a) The Land and Agriculture
(b) The People
(c) The Policy of Socialism and Self-Reliance, and
(d) Good Leadership.

### (a) *The Land*

Because the economy of Tanzania depends and will continue to depend on agriculture and animal husbandry, Tanzanians can live well without depending on help from outside if they use their land properly. Land is the basis of human life and all Tanzanians should use it as a valuable investment for future development. Because the land belongs to the nation, the Government has to see to it that it is used for the benefit of the whole nation and not for the benefit of one individual or just a few people.

It is the responsibility of TANU to see that the country produces enough food and enough cash crops for export. It is the responsibility of the Government and the co-operative societies to see to it that our people get the necessary tools, training and leadership in modern methods of agriculture.

### (b) *The People*

In order properly to implement the policy of self-reliance, the people have to be taught the meaning of self-reliance and its practice. They must become self-sufficient in food, serviceable clothes and good housing.

In our country work should be something to be
proud of, and laziness, drunkenness and idleness should
be things to be ashamed of. And for the defence of our
nation, it is necessary for us to be on guard against
internal stooges who could be used by external enemies
who aim to destroy us. The people should always be
ready to defend their nation when they are called upon to
do so.

### (c) *Good Policies*

The principles of our policy of self-reliance go hand in
hand with our policy on socialism. In order to prevent
exploitation it is necessary for everybody to work and to
live on his own labour. And in order to distribute the
national wealth fairly, it is necessary for everybody to work
to the maximum of his ability. Nobody should go and stay
for a long time with his relative, doing no work, because in
doing so he will be exploiting his relative. Likewise,
nobody should be allowed to loiter in towns or villages without doing work which would enable him to be self-reliant
without exploiting his relatives.

TANU believes that everybody who loves his nation has
a duty to serve it by co-operating with his fellows in building
the country for the benefit of all the people of Tanzania.
In order to maintain our independence and our people's
freedom we ought to be self-reliant in every possible way
and avoid depending upon other countries for assistance.
If every individual is self-reliant the ten-house cell
will be self-reliant; if all the cells are self-reliant the
whole ward will be self-reliant; and if the wards are
self-reliant the District will be self-reliant. If the Districts
are self-reliant, then the Region is self-reliant, and if the
Regions are self-reliant, then the whole nation is self-reliant
and this our aim.

(d) *Good Leadership*

TANU recognizes the urgency and importance of good leadership. But we have not yet produced systematic training for our leaders; it is necessary that TANU Headquarters should now prepare a programme of training for all leaders—from the national level to the ten-house cell level —so that every one of them understands our political and economic policies. Leaders must set a good example to the rest of the people in their lives and in all their activities.

## PART FOUR

### TANU Membership

Since the Party was founded we have put great emphasis on getting as many members as possible. This was the right policy during the independence struggle. But now the National Executive feels that the time has come when we should put more emphasis on the beliefs of our Party and its policies of socialism.

That part of the TANU Constitution which relates to the admission of a member should be adhered to, and if it is discovered that a man does not appear to accept the faith, the objects, and the rules and regulations of the Party, then he should not be accepted as a member. In particular, it should not be forgotten that TANU is a Party of peasants and workers.

## PART FIVE

### The Arusha Resolution

Therefore, the National Executive Committee, meeting in the Community Centre at Arusha from 26.1.67 to 29.1.67 resolves:

(a) *The Leadership*
1. Every TANU and Government leader must be either a peasant or a worker, and should in no way be associated with the practices of capitalism or feudalism.
2. No TANU or Government leader should hold shares in any company.
3. No TANU or Government leader should hold directorships in any privately owned enterprise.
4. No TANU or Government leader should receive two or more salaries.
5. No TANU or Government leader should own houses which he rents to others.
6. For the purposes of this Resolution the term 'leader' should comprise the following:

   Members of the TANU National Executive Committee; Ministers; Members of Parliament; senior officials of organizations affiliated to TANU; senior officials of para-statal organizations; all those appointed or elected under any clause of the TANU Constitution; councillors; and civil servants in the high and middle cadres. (In this context 'leader' means a man, or a man and his wife; a woman, or a woman and her husband.)

(b) *The Government and other Institutions*
1. Congratulates the Government for the steps it has taken so far in the implementation of the policy of socialism.
2. Calls upon the Government to take further steps in the implementation of our policy of socialism as described in Part Two of this document without waiting for a Presidential Commission on Socialism.
3. Calls upon the Government to put emphasis, when preparing its development plans, on the ability of this country to implement the plans rather than depending on

foreign loans and grants as has been done in the current Five-Year Development Plan. The National Executive Committee also resolves that the Plan should be amended so as to make it fit in with the policy of self-reliance.

4. Calls upon the Government to take action designed to ensure that the incomes of workers in the private sector are not very different from the incomes of workers in the public sector.

5. Calls upon the Government to put great emphasis on actions which will raise the standard of living of the peasants, and the rural community.

6. Calls upon NUTA, the co-operatives, TAPA, UWT, TYL, and other Government institutions to take steps to implement the policy of socialism and self-reliance.

(c) *Membership*

Members should get thorough teaching on Party ideology so that they may understand it, and they should always be reminded of the importance of living up to its principles.

# 3

# Socialism is not Racialism

*Printed in* The Nationalist, *14 February 1967*

The Arusha Declaration and the actions relating to public ownership which we took last week were all concerned with ensuring that we can build socialism in our country. The nationalization and the taking of a controlling interest in many firms were a necessary part of our determination to organize our society in such a way that our efforts benefit all our people and that there is no exploitation of one man by another.

Yet these actions do not in themselves create socialism. They are necessary to it, but as the Arusha Declaration states, they could also be the basis for fascism—in other words, for the oppressive extreme of capitalism. For the words with which I began my pamphlet 'Ujamaa' in 1962 remain valid; socialism is an attitude of mind. The basis of socialism is a belief in the oneness of man and the common historical destiny of mankind. Its basis, in other words, is human equality.

Acceptance of this principle is absolutely fundamental to socialism. The justification of socialism is man; not the state, not the flag. Socialism is not for the benefit of black men, nor brown men, nor white men, nor yellow men. The purpose of socialism is the service of man, regardless of colour, size, shape, skill, ability, or anything else. And the economic institutions of socialism, such as those we are now creating in accordance with the Arusha Declaration, are intended to serve man in our society. Where the majority c f the people in a particular society are black, then most of

those who benefit from socialism there will be black. But
it has nothing to do with their blackness; only with their
humanity.

Some years ago I made the point that fascism and racialism can go together, but socialism and racialism are incompatible. The reason is easy to see. Fascism is the highest
and most ruthless form of the exploitation of man by man;
it is made possible by deliberate efforts to divide mankind
and set one group of men against another group.

In Nazi Germany the majority were incited to join in hos-
tile actions against the Jews—who were a minority religious
and ethnic group living among them. 'I hate Jews' became
the basis of life for supporters of the Nazi government.

But the man or woman who hates 'Jews', or 'Asians', or
'Europeans', or even 'West Europeans and Americans'
is not a socialist. He is trying to divide mankind into groups
and is judging men according to the skin colour and shape
they were given by God. Or he is dividing men according
to national boundaries. In either case he is denying the
equality and brotherhood of man.

Without an acceptance of human equality there can be no
socialism. This is true however 'socialist' the institutions
may be. Thus it was that when Nazi Germany organized
the Krupp group of industries no socialist could rejoice;
for it simply meant that the fascist state was more highly
organized than ever. Nor do socialists welcome the news
that South Africa has established an oil trading and refining
company in which the state owns a controlling interest.
We know that this simply makes that fascist state more
efficient in its oppression and more able to defend itself
against attack.

We in Tanzania have to hold fast to this lesson, especially
now as we advance on the socialist road. For it is true that
because of our colonial history the vast majority of the

capitalist organizations in this country are owned and run
by Asians or by Western Europeans. Twenty years ago we
could have said all the capitalists in this country were from
those areas; we cannot say this now. For the truth is that
capitalism and capitalist attitudes have nothing whatsoever
to do with the race or national origin of those who believe
in them or practise them. Indeed, nobody who was at
Arusha needs any more proof that the temptations of
capitalism ignore colour boundaries. Even leaders of TANU
were getting deeply involved in the practices of capitalism
and landlordism. A few had started talking of 'my
Company'. And very many others would have done so
if they could; they were capitalists by desire even when
they could not be so in practice. Hence the resolution on
leadership. Hence the difficulties we must expect in en-
forcing this resolution.

Socialism has nothing to do with race, nor with country
of origin. In fact any intelligent man, whether he is a
socialist or not, realizes that there are socialists in capitalist
countries—and from capitalist countries. Very often such
socialists come to work in newly independent and avowedly
socialist countries like Tanzania, because they are frustrated
in their capitalist homeland. Neither is any intelligent man
blind to the fact that there are frustrated capitalists in the
communist countries—just as there will in time be frustrated
capitalists in Tanzania. It may even be that some of those
frustrated capitalists from Eastern countries come to work
with us.

Neither is it sensible for a socialist to talk as if all capitalists are devils. It is one thing to dislike the capitalist
system, and to try and frustrate people's capitalist desires.
But it would be as stupid for us to assume that capitalists
have horns as it is for people in Western Europe to assume
that we in Tanzania have become devils.

In fact the leaders in the capitalist countries have now begun to realize that communists are human beings like themselves—that they are not devils. One day they will realize that this includes the Chinese communists! It would be very absurd if we react to the stupidity they are growing out of, and become equally stupid ourselves in the opposite direction! We have to recognize in our words and our actions that capitalists are human beings just as social- ists are. They may be wrong; indeed by dedicating our- selves to socialism we are saying that they are. But our task is to make it impossible for capitalism to dominate us. Our task is not to persecute capitalists or make dignified life impossible for those who would be capitalists if they could.

In truth it is necessary for socialists to think about issues —about policies—and about how our institutions can serve the people of our society. To try and divide up the people working for our nation into groups of 'good' and 'bad' according to their skin colour, or their national origin, or their tribal origin, is to sabotage the work we have just embarked upon. We should decide whether a person is efficient in a particular job, whether he is honest, and whether he is carrying out his task loyally. But those of us who call ourselves scientific socialists must be scientific and objective in our thinking and in making such judge- ments. We must think about men, and an individual man, not about 'Asians', 'Europeans', 'Americans', and so on.

Certainly socialism in Tanzania will be built by Tanzanians. And certainly we are working for the time when all those in our Government employment will be Tanzanians—although they will not all be black Tanzanians. But it is absurd for anyone to suggest that because we now have non-Tanzanians working for Government—or in the newly nationalized industries—that we do not control our

own affairs. Only those who are lacking in self-confidence,
or who are trying to hide their own shortcomings, could
say this now. For all the evidence is against them. We
obtained our independence although we were governed by
colonialists. We became a Republic although there were
many expatriates working here—at that time even in high
positions. We effected the Union of Tanganyika and Zanzibar although many Government servants on the mainland
came from countries which did not like the Zanzibar Revolution. We have accepted the Arusha Declaration, and in
the space of one week have nationalized or taken control
of all the large capitalist firms and institutions which could
have dominated our economy. In all these activities we
have used all the Government servants concerned. And
all—Tanzanians and non-Tanzanians alike—are carrying
out our decisions loyally, and are working very hard
indeed.

The Arusha Declaration talks of men, and their beliefs.
It talks of socialism and capitalism, of socialists and capitalists. It does not talk about racial groups or nationalities.
On the contrary, it says that all those who stand for the
interests of the workers and peasants, anywhere in the
world, are our friends. This means that we must judge the
character and ability of each individual, not put each
person into a pre-arranged category of race or national
origin and judge them accordingly. Certainly no one can
be a socialist unless he at least tries to do this. For if the
actions taken under the Arusha Declaration are to mean
anything to our people, then we must accept this basic
oneness of man. What matters now is that we should
succeed in the work we have undertaken. The colour or
origin of the man who is working to that end does not
matter in the very least. And each one of us must fight,
in himself, the racialist habits of thought which were part

of our inheritance from colonialism.

It is not an easy thing to overcome such habits. But we have always known that it is necessary, and that racialism is evil. We fought our independence campaign on that basis. And the equality of man is the first item in the TANU Creed. For in our Constitution we say, 'TANU believes (a) That all human beings are equal; (b) That every individual has a right to dignity and respect'.

If we are to succeed in building a socialist state in this country it is essential that every citizen, and especially every TANU leader, should live up to that doctrine. Let us always remember two things. We have dedicated ourselves to build a socialist society in Tanzania. And, socialism and racialism are incompatible.

# 4

# Education for Self-Reliance

*Policy booklet published in March 1967*

Since long before independence the people of this country, under the leadership of TANU, have been demanding more education for their children. But we have never really stopped to consider why we want education—what its purpose is. Therefore, although over time there have been various criticisms about the details of curricula provided in schools, we have not until now questioned the basic system of education which we took over at the time of independence. We have never done that because we have never thought about education except in terms of obtaining teachers, engineers, administrators, etc. Individually and collectively we have in practice thought of education as a training for the skills required to earn high salaries in the modern sector of our economy.

It is now time that we looked again at the justification for a poor society like ours spending almost 20 per cent of its Government revenues on providing education for its children and young people, and began to consider what that education should be doing. For in our circumstances it is impossible to devote Shs. 147,330,000/- every year to education for some of our children (while others go without) unless its result has a proportionate relevance to the society we are trying to create.

The educational systems in different kinds of societies in the world have been, and are, very different in organization and in content. They are different because the societies providing the education are different, and because education, whether it be formal or informal, has a purpose. That purpose is to transmit from one generation to the next the accumulated wisdom and knowledge of the society, and to prepare the young people for their future membership of the society and their active participation in its maintenance or development.

This is true, explicitly or implicitly, for all societies—the capitalist societies of the West, the communist societies of the East, and the pre-colonial African societies too.

The fact that pre-colonial Africa did not have 'schools'—except for short periods of initiation in some tribes—did not mean that the children were not educated. They learned by living and doing. In the homes and on the farms they were taught the skills of the society, and the behaviour expected of its members. They learned the kind of grasses which were suitable for which purposes, the work which had to be done on the crops, or the care which had to be given to animals, by joining with their elders in this work. They learned the tribal history, and the tribe's relationship with other tribes and with the spirits, by listening to the stories of the elders. Through these means, and by the custom of sharing to which young people were taught to conform, the values of the society were transmitted. Education was thus 'informal'; every adult was a teacher to a greater or lesser degree  But this lack of formality did not mean that there was no education, nor did it affect its importance to the society. Indeed, it may have made the education more directly relevant to the society in which the child was growing up.

In Europe education has been formalized for a very long time. An examination of its development will show, however, that it has always had similar objectives to those implicit in the traditional African system of education.

That is to say, formal education in Europe was intended to reinforce the social ethics existing in the particular country, and to prepare the children and young people for the place they will have in that society. The same thing is true of communist countries now. The content of education is somewhat different from that of Western countries, but the purpose is the same—to prepare young people to live in and to serve the society, and to transmit the knowledge, skills, and values and attitudes of the society. Wherever education fails in any of these fields, then the society falters in its progress, or there is social unrest as people find that their education has prepared them for a future which is not open to them.

## Colonial Education in Tanzania and the Inheritance of the New State

The education provided by the colonial government in the two countries which now form Tanzania had a different purpose. It was not designed to prepare young people for the service of their own country; instead it was motivated by a desire to inculcate the values of the colonial society and to train individuals for the service of the colonial state. In these countries the state interest in education therefore stemmed from the need for local clerks and junior officials; on top of that, various religious groups were interested in spreading literacy and other education as part of their evangelical work.

This statement of fact is not given as a criticism of the many individuals who worked hard, often under difficult conditions, in teaching and in organizing educational work. Nor does it imply that all the values these people transmitted in the schools were wrong or inappropriate. What it does mean, however, is that the educational system introduced into Tanzania by the colonialists was modelled on the British system, but with even heavier emphasis on subservient attitudes and on white-collar skills. Inevitably, too, it was based on the assumptions of a colonialist and capitalist society. It emphasized and encouraged the individualistic instincts of mankind, instead of his co-operative instincts. It led to the possession of individual material wealth being the major criterion of social merit and worth.

This meant that colonial education induced attitudes of human inequality, and in practice underpinned the domination of the weak by the strong, especially in the economic field. Colonial education in this country was therefore not transmitting the values and knowledge of Tanzanian society from one generation to the next; it was a deliberate attempt to change those values and to replace traditional knowledge by the knowledge from a different society. It was thus a part of a deliberate attempt to effect a revolution in the society; to make it into a colonial society which accepted its status and which was an efficient adjunct to the governing power. Its failure to achieve these ends does not mean that it was without an influence on the attitudes, ideas, and knowledge of the people who experienced it. Nor does that failure imply that the education provided in colonial days is automatically relevant for the purposes of a free people committed to the principle of equality.

The independent state of Tanzania in fact inherited a system of education which was in many respects both inadequate and inappropriate for the new state. It was, however, its inadequacy which was most immediately obvious. So little education had been provided that in December, 1961, we had too few people with the necessary educational qualifications even to man the administration

of Government as it was then, much less undertake the big
economic and social development work which was essential.
Neither was the school population in 1961 large enough
to allow for any expectation that this situation would be
speedily corrected. On top of that, education was based
upon race, whereas the whole moral case of the independence movement had been based upon a rejection of racial
distinctions.

## Action since Independence

The three most glaring faults of the educational inheritance
have already been tackled. First, the racial distinctions
within education were abolished. Complete integration
of the separate racial systems was introduced very soon
after independence, and discrimination on grounds of
religion was also brought to an end. A child in Tanzania
can now secure admittance to any Government or Govern-
ment-aided school in this country without regard to his
race or religion and without fear that he will be subject
to religious indoctrination as the price of learning.

Secondly, there has been a very big expansion of educational facilities available, especially at the secondary school
and post-secondary school levels. In 1961 there were
490,000 children attending primary schools in Tanganyika,
the majority of them only going up to Standard IV. In
1967 there were 825,000 children attending such schools,
and increasingly these will be full seven-year primary schools.
In 1961, too, there were 11,832 children in secondary schools,
only 176 of whom were in Form VI. This year there are
25,000 and 830. This is certainly something for our young
state to be proud of. It is worth reminding ourselves that
our present problems (especially the so-called problem
of the primary school leavers) are revealing themselves
largely because of these successes.

The third action we have taken is to make the education provided in all our schools much more Tanzanian in content. No longer do our children simply learn British and European history. Faster than would have been thought possible our University College and other institutions are providing materials on the history of Africa and making these available to our teachers. Our national songs and dances are once again being learned by our children; our national language has been given the importance in our curriculum which it needs and deserves. Also, civics classes taken by Tanzanians are beginning to give the secondary school pupils an understanding of the organization and aims of our young state. In these and other ways changes have been introduced to make our educational system more relevant to our needs. At this time, when there is so much general and justified questioning of what is being done, it is appropriate that we should pay tribute to the work of our teachers and those who support their work in the Ministry, in the Institute of Education, the University College and the District Councils.

Yet all these things I have mentioned are modifications of the system we have inherited. Their results have not yet been seen; it takes years for a change in education to have its effect. The events of 1966 do suggest, however, that a more thorough examination of the education we are providing must be made. It is now clearly time for us to think seriously about this question: 'What is the educational system in Tanzania intended to do—what is its purpose?' Having decided that, we have to look at the relevance of the existing structure and content of Tanzanian education for the task it has to do. In the light of that examination we can consider whether, in our present circumstances, further modifications are required or whether we need a change in the whole approach.

*What kind of Society are we trying to build?*

Only when we are clear about the kind of society we are trying to build can we design our educational service to serve our goals. But this is not now a problem in Tanzania. Although we do not claim to have drawn up a blueprint of the future, the values and objectives of our society have been stated many times. We have said that we want to create a socialist society which is based on three principles: equality and respect for human dignity; sharing of the resources which are produced by our efforts; work by everyone and exploitation by none. We have set out these ideas clearly in the National Ethic; and in the Arusha Declaration and earlier documents we have outlined the principles and policies we intend to follow. We have also said on many occasions that our objective is greater African unity, and that we shall work for this objective while in the meantime defending the absolute integrity and sovereignty of the United Republic. Most often of all, our Government and people have stressed the equality of all citizens, and our determination that economic, political, and social policies shall be deliberately designed to make a reality of that equality in all spheres of life. We are, in other words, committed to a socialist future and one in which the people will themselves determine the policies pursued by a Government which is responsible to them.

It is obvious, however, that if we are to make progress towards these goals, we in Tanzania must accept the realities of our present position, internally and externally, and then work to change these realities into something more in accord with our desires. And the truth is that our United Republic has at present a poor, undeveloped, and agricultural economy. We have very little capital to invest in big factories or modern machines; we are short of people with skill and experience. What we do have is land in abundance and people who are willing to work hard for their own improvement. It is the use of these latter resources which will decide whether we reach our total goals or not. If we use these resources in a spirit of self-reliance as the basis for development, then we shall make progress slowly but surely. And it will then be real progress, affecting the lives of the masses, not just having spectacular show-pieces in the towns while the rest of the people of Tanzania live in their present poverty.

Pursuing this path means that Tanzania will continue to have a predominantly rural economy for a long time to come. And as it is in the rural areas that people live and work, so it is in the rural areas that life must be improved. This is not to say that we shall have no industries and factories in the near future. We have some now and they will continue to expand. But it would be grossly unrealistic to imagine that in the near future more than a small proportion of our people will live in towns and work in modern industrial enterprises. It is therefore the villages which must be made into places where people live a good life; it is in the rural areas that people must be able to find their material well-being and their satisfactions.

This improvement in village life will not, however, come automatically. It will come only if we pursue a deliberate policy of using the resources we have—our manpower and our land—to the best advantage. This means people working hard, intelligently, and together; in other words, working in co-operation. Our people in the rural areas, as well as their Government, must organize themselves co-operatively and work for themselves through working for the community of which they are members. Our village life, as well as our state organization, must be based on the principles of socialism and that equality in work and return which is part of it.

This is what our educational system has to encourage. It has to foster the social goals of living together, and working together, for the common good. It has to prepare our young people to play a dynamic and constructive part in the development of a society in which all members share fairly in the good or bad fortune of the group, and in which progress is measured in terms of human well-being, not prestige buildings, cars, or other such things, whether privately or publicly owned. Our education must therefore inculcate a sense of commitment to the total community, and help the pupils to accept the values appropriate to our kind of future, not those appropriate to our colonial past.

This means that the educational system of Tanzania must emphasize co-operative endeavour, not individual advancement; it must stress concepts of equality and the responsibility to give service which goes with any special ability, whether it be in carpentry, in animal husbandry, or in academic pursuits. And, in particular, our education must counteract the temptation to intellectual arrogance; for this leads to the well-educated despising those whose abilities are non-academic or who have no special abilities but are just human beings. Such arrogance has no place in a society of equal citizens.

It is, however, not only in relation to social values that our educational system has a task to do. It must also prepare young people for the work they will be called upon to do in the society which exists in Tanzania—a rural society where improvement will depend largely upon the efforts of the people in agriculture and in village development. This does not mean that education in Tanzania should be designed just to produce passive agricultural workers of different levels of skill who simply carry out plans or directions received from above. It must produce good farmers; it has also to prepare people for their responsibilities as free workers and citizens in a free and democratic society, albeit a largely rural society. They have to be able to think for themselves, to make judgements on all the issues affecting them; they have to be able to interpret the decisions made through the democratic institutions of our society, and to implement them in the light of the peculiar local circumstances where they happen to live.

It would thus be a gross misinterpretation of our needs to suggest that the educational system should be designed to produce robots, who work hard but never question what the leaders in Government or TANU are doing and saying. For the people are, and must be, Government and TANU. Our Government and our Party must always be responsible to the people, and must always consist of representatives— spokesmen and servants of the people. The education provided must therefore encourage the development in each citizen of three things: an enquiring mind; an ability to learn from what others do, and reject or adapt it to his own needs; and a basic confidence in his own position as a free and equal member of the society, who values others and is valued by them for what he does and not for what he obtains.

These things are important for both the vocational and the social aspects of education. However much agriculture a young person learns, he will not find a book which will give him all the answers to all the detailed problems he will come across on his own farm. He will have to learn the basic principles of modern knowledge in agriculture and then adapt them to solve his own problems. Similarly, the free citizens of Tanzania will have to judge social issues for themselves; there neither is, nor will be, a political 'holy book' which purports to give all the answers to all the social, political and economic problems which will face our country in the future. There will be philosophies and policies approved by our society which citizens should consider and apply in the light of their own thinking and experience. But the educational system of Tanzania would not be serving the interests of a democratic socialist society if it tried to stop people from thinking about the teachings, policies or the beliefs of leaders, either past or present. Only free people conscious of their worth and their equality can build a free society.

## Some Salient Features of the Existing Educational System

These are very different purposes from those which are promoted by our existing educational arrangements. For there are four basic elements in the present system which prevent, or at least discourage, the integration of the pupils into the society they will enter, and which do encourage attitudes of inequality, intellectual arrogance and intense individualism among the young people who go through our schools.

First, the most central thing about the education we are at present providing is that it is basically an elitist education designed to meet the interests and needs of a very small proportion of those who enter the school system.

Although only about 13 per cent of our primary school children will get a place in a secondary school, the basis of our primary school education is the preparation of pupils for secondary schools. Thus 87 per cent of the children who finished primary school last year—and a similar proportion of those who will finish this year—do so with a sense of failure, of a legitimate aspiration having been denied them. Indeed we all speak in these terms, by referring to them as those who failed to enter secondary schools, instead of simply as those who have finished their primary education. On the other hand, the other 13 per cent have a feeling of having deserved a prize—and the prize they and their parents now expect is high wages, comfortable employment in towns, and personal status in the society. The same process operates again at the next highest level, when entrance to university is the question at issue.

In other words, the education now provided is designed for the few who are intellectually stronger than their fellows; it induces among those who succeed a feeling of superiority, and leaves the majority of the others hankering after something they will never obtain. It induces a feeling of inferiority among the majority, and can thus not produce either the egalitarian society we should build, nor the attitudes of mind which are conducive to an egalitarian society. On the contrary, it induces the growth of a class structure in our country.

Equally important is the second point; the fact that Tanzania's education is such as to divorce its participants from the society it is supposed to be preparing them for. This is particularly true of secondary schools, which are inevitably almost entirely boarding schools; but to some extent, and despite recent modifications in the curriculum, it is true of primary schools too. We take children from their parents at the age of 7 years, and for up to $7\frac{1}{2}$ hours a day we teach them certain basic academic skills. In recent years we have tried to relate these skills, at least in theory, to the life which the children see around them. But the school is always separate; it is not part of the society. It is a place children go to and which they and their parents hope will make it unnecessary for them to become farmers and continue living in the villages.

The few who go to secondary schools are taken many miles away from their homes; they live in an enclave, having permission to go into the town for recreation, but not relating the work of either town or country to their real life—which is lived in the school compound. Later a few people go to university. If they are lucky enough to enter Dar es Salaam University College they live in comfortable quarters, feed well, and study hard for their degree. When they have been successful in obtaining it, they know immediately that they will receive a salary of something like £660 per annum. That is what they have been aiming for; it is what they have been encouraged to aim for. They may also have the desire to serve the community, but their idea of service is related to status and the salary which a university education is expected to confer upon its recipient. The salary and the status have become a right automatically conferred by the degree.

It is wrong of us to criticize the young people for these attitudes. The new university graduate has spent the larger part of his life separated and apart from the masses of Tanzania; his parents may be poor, but he has never fully shared that poverty. He does not really know what it is like to live as a poor peasant. He will be more at home in the world of the educated than he is among his own parents. Only during vacations has he spent time at home, and even then he will often find that his parents and relatives support his own conception of his difference, and regard it as wrong that he should live and work as the ordinary person he really is. For the truth is that many of the people in Tanzania have come to regard education as meaning that a man is too precious for the rough and hard life which the masses of our people still live.

The third point is that our present system encourages school pupils in the idea that all knowledge which is worthwhile is acquired from books or from 'educated people'—meaning those who have been through a formal education. The knowledge and wisdom of other old people is despised, and they themselves regarded as being ignorant and of no account. Indeed it is not only the education system which at present has this effect. Government and Party themselves tend to judge people according to whether they have 'passed school certificate', 'have a degree', etc. If a man has these qualifications we assume he can fill a post; we do not wait to find out about his attitudes, his character, or any other ability except the ability to pass examinations. If a man does not have these qualifications we assume he cannot do a job; we ignore his knowledge and experience. For example, I recently visited a very good tobacco-producing peasant. But if I tried to take him into Government as a Tobacco Extension Officer, I would run up against the system because he has no formal education. Everything we do stresses book learning, and underestimates the value to our society of traditional knowledge and the wisdom which is often acquired by intelligent men and women as they experience life, even without their being able to read at all.

This does not mean that any person can do any job simply because they are old and wise, nor that educational qualifications are not necessary. This is a mistake our people sometimes fall into as a reaction against the arrogance of the book-learned. A man is not necessarily wise because he is old; a man cannot necessarily run a factory because he has been working in it as a labourer or storekeeper for 20 years. But equally he may not be able to do so if he has a Doctorate in Commerce. The former may have honesty and ability to weigh up men; the latter may have the ability to initiate a transaction and work out the economics of it. But both qualifications are necessary in one man if the factory is to be a successful and modern enterprise serving our nation. It is as much a mistake to over-value book learning as it is to under-value it.

The same thing applies in relation to agricultural knowledge. Our farmers have been on the land for a long time. The methods they use are the result of long experience in the struggle with nature; even the rules and taboos they honour have a basis in reason. It is not enough to abuse a traditional farmer as old-fashioned; we must try to understand why he is doing certain things, and not just assume he is stupid. But this does not mean that his methods are sufficient for the future. The traditional systems may have been appropriate for the economy which existed when they were worked out and for the technical knowledge then available. But different tools and different land tenure systems are being used now; land should no longer be used for a year or two and then abandoned for up to 20 years to give time for natural regeneration to take place. The introduction of an ox-plough instead of a hoe—and, even more, the introduction of a tractor—means more than just a different way of turning over the land. It requires a change in the organization of work, both to see that the maximum advantage is taken of the new tool, and also to see that the new method does not simply lead to the rapid destruction of our land and the egalitarian basis of our society. Again, therefore, our young people have to learn both a practical respect for the knowledge of the old 'uneducated' farmer, and an understanding of new methods and the reason for them.

Yet at present our pupils learn to despise even their own parents because they are old-fashioned and ignorant; there is nothing in our existing educational system which suggests to the pupil that he can learn important things about farming from his elders. The result is that he absorbs beliefs about witchcraft before he goes to school, but does not learn the properties of local grasses; he absorbs the taboos from his family but does not learn the methods of making nutritious traditional foods. And from school he acquires knowledge unrelated to agricultural life. He gets the worst of both systems!

Finally, and in some ways most importantly, our young and poor nation is taking out of productive work some of its healthiest and strongest young men and women. Not only do they fail to contribute to that increase in output which is so urgent for our nation; they themselves consume the output of the older and often weaker people. There are almost 25,000 students in secondary schools now; they do not learn as they work, they simply learn. What is more, they take it for granted that this should be so. Whereas in a wealthy country like the United States of America it is common for young people to work their way through high school and college, in Tanzania the structure of our education makes it impossible for them to do so. Even during the holidays we assume that these young men and women should be protected from rough work; neither they nor the community expect them to spend their time on hard physical labour or on jobs which are uncomfortable and unpleasant. This is not simply a reflection of the fact that there are many people looking for unskilled paid employment—pay is not the question at issue. It is a reflection of the attitude we have all adopted.

How many of our students spend their vacations doing a job which could improve people's lives but for which there is no money—jobs like digging an irrigation channel or a drainage ditch for a village, or demonstrating the construction and explaining the benefits of deep-pit latrines, and so on? A small number have done such work in the National Youth Camps or through school-organized, nation-building schemes, but they are the exception rather than the rule. The vast majority do not think of their knowledge or their strength as being related to the needs of the village community.

*Can these Faults be corrected?*

There are three major aspects which require attention if this situation is to change: the content of the curriculum itself, the organization of the schools, and the entry age into primary schools. But although these aspects are in some ways separate, they are also inter-locked. We cannot integrate the pupils and students into the future society simply by theoretical teaching, however well designed it is. Neither can the society fully benefit from an education system which is thoroughly integrated into local life but does not teach people the basic skills—for example, of literacy and arithmetic, or which fails to excite in them a curiosity about ideas. Nor can we expect those finishing primary school to be useful young citizens if they are still only 12 or 13 years of age.

In considering changes in the present structure it is also essential that we face the facts of our present economic situation. Every penny spent on education is money taken away from some other needed activity—whether it is an investment in the future, better medical services, or just more food, clothing and comfort for our citizens at present. And the truth is that there is no possibility of Tanzania being able to increase the proportion of the national income which is spent on education; it ought to be decreased. Therefore we cannot solve our present problems by any solution which costs more than is at present spent; in particular we cannot solve the 'problem of primary school leavers' by increasing the number of secondary school places.

This 'problem of primary school leavers' is in fact a product of the present system. Increasingly children are starting school at 6 or even 5 years of age, so that they finish primary school when they are still too young to become responsible young workers and citizens. On top of that is the fact that both the society and the type of education they have received led them to expect wage employment—probably in an office. In other words, their education was not sufficiently related to the tasks which have to be done in our society. This problem therefore calls for a major change in the content of our primary education and for the raising of the primary school entry age so that the child is older when he leaves, and also able to learn more quickly while he is at school.

There is no other way in which this problem of primary school leavers can be solved. Unpleasant though it may be, the fact is that it is going to be a long time before we can provide universal primary education in Tanzania; for the vast majority of those who do get this opportunity, it will be only the equivalent of the present seven years' education. It is only a few who will have the chance of going on to secondary schools, and quite soon only a proportion of these who will have an opportunity of going on to university, even if they can benefit from doing so. These are the economic facts of life for our country. They are the practical meaning of our poverty. The only choice before us is how we allocate the educational opportunities, and whether we emphasize the individual interests of the few or whether we design our educational system to serve the community as a whole. And for a socialist state only the latter is really possible.

The implication of this is that the education given in our primary schools must be a complete education in itself. It must not continue to be simply a preparation for secondary school. Instead of the primary school activities being geared to the competitive examination which will select the few who go on to secondary school, they must be a preparation for the life which the majority of the children will lead. Similarly, secondary schools must not be simply

a selection process for the university, teachers' colleges,
and so on. They must prepare people for life and service
in the villages and rural areas of this country. For in
Tanzania the only true justification for secondary education
is that it is needed by the few for service to the many. The
teacher in a seven-year primary school system needs an
education which goes beyond seven years; the extension
officer who will help a population with a seven-years'
education needs a lot more himself. Other essential services
need higher education—for example, doctors and engineers
need long and careful training. But publicly provided
'education for education's sake' must be general education
for the masses. Further education for a selected few must
be education for service to the many. There can be no
other justification for taxing the many to give education
to only a few.

Yet it is easy to say that our primary and secondary
schools must prepare young people for the realities and
needs of Tanzania; to do it requires a radical change, not
only in the education system but also in many existing
community attitudes. In particular, it requires that examinations should be down-graded in Government and
public esteem. We have to recognize that although they
have certain advantages—for example, in reducing the
dangers of nepotism and tribalism in a selection process—
they also have severe disadvantages too. As a general
rule they assess a person's ability to learn facts and present
them on demand within a time period. They do not always
succeed in assessing a power to reason, and they certainly
do not assess character or willingness to serve.

Further, at the present time our curriculum and syllabus
are geared to the examinations set—only to a very limited
extent does the reverse situation apply. A teacher who is
trying to help his pupils often studies the examination papers

for past years and judges what questions are most likely to be asked next time; he then concentrates his teaching on those matters, knowing that by doing so he is giving his children the best chance of getting through to secondary school or university. And the examinations our children at present sit are themselves geared to an international standard and practice which has developed regardless of our particular problems and need. What we need to do now is think first about the education we want to provide, and when that thinking is completed think about whether some form of examination is an appropriate way of closing an education phase. Then such an examination should be designed to fit the education which has been provided.

Most important of all is that we should change the things we demand of our schools. We should not determine the type of things children are taught in primary schools by the things a doctor, engineer, teacher, economist, or administrator need to know. Most of our pupils will never be any of these things. We should determine the type of things taught in the primary schools by the things which the boy or girl ought to know—that is, the skills he ought to acquire and the values he ought to cherish if he, or she, is to live happily and well in a socialist and predominantly rural society, and contribute to the improvement of life there. Our sights must be on the majority; it is they we must be aiming at in determining the curriculum and syllabus. Those most suitable for further education will still become obvious, and they will not suffer. For the purpose is not to provide an inferior education to that given at present. The purpose is to provide a different education —one realistically designed to fulfil the common purposes of education in the particular society of Tanzania. The same thing must be true at post-primary schools. The object of the teaching must be the provision of knowledge, skills and attitudes which will serve the student when he or she lives and works in a developing and changing socialist state; it must not be aimed at university entrance.

Alongside this change in the approach to the curriculum there must be a parallel and integrated change in the way our schools are run, so as to make them and their inhabitants a real part of our society and our economy. Schools must, in fact, become communities—and communities which practise the precept of self-reliance. The teachers, workers, and pupils together must be the members of a social unit in the same way as parents, relatives, and children are the family social unit. There must be the same kind of relationship between pupils and teachers within the school community as there is between children and parents in the village. And the former community must realize, just as the latter do, that their life and well-being depend upon the production of wealth—by farming or other activities. This means that all schools, but especially secondary schools and other forms of higher education, must contribute to their own upkeep; they must be economic communities as well as social and educational communities. Each school should have, as an integral part of it, a farm or workshop which provides the food eaten by the community, and makes some contribution to the total national income.

This is not a suggestion that a school farm or workshop should be attached to every school for training purposes. It is a suggestion that every school should also be a farm; that the school community should consist of people who are both teachers and farmers, and pupils and farmers. Obviously if there is a school farm, the pupils working on it should be learning the techniques and tasks of farming. But the farm would be an integral part of the school—and the welfare of the pupils would depend on its output, just as the welfare of a farmer depends on the output of his land. Thus, when this scheme is in operation, the revenue side of school accounts would not just read as at present—'Grant from Government...; Grant from voluntary agency or other charity...'. They would read—'Income from sale of cotton (or whatever other cash crop was appropriate for the area) ...; Value of the food grown and consumed ...; Value of labour done by pupils on new building, repairs, equipment, etc....; Government subvention...; Grant from ...'.

This is a break with our educational tradition, and unless its purpose and its possibilities are fully understood by teachers and parents, it may be resented at the beginning. But the truth is that it is not a regressive measure, nor a punishment either for teachers or pupils. It is a recognition that we in Tanzania have to work our way out of poverty, and that we are all members of the one society, depending upon each other. There will be difficulties of implementation, especially at first. For example, we do not now have a host of experienced farm managers who could be used as planners and teachers on the new school farms. But this is not an insuperable difficulty; and certainly life will not halt in Tanzania until we get experienced farm managers. Life and farming will go on as we train. Indeed, by using good local farmers as supervisors and teachers of particular aspects of the work, and using the services of the agricultural officers and assistants, we shall be helping to break down the notion that only book learning is worthy of respect. This is an important element in our socialist development.

Neither does this concept of schools contributing to their own upkeep simply mean using our children as labourers who follow traditional methods. On the contrary, on a school farm pupils can learn by doing. The important place of the hoe and of other simple tools can be demon-

strated; the advantages of improved seeds, of simple ox-
ploughs, and of proper methods of animal husbandry
can become obvious; and the pupils can learn by practice
how to use these things to the best advantage. The farm
work and products should be integrated into the school
life; thus the properties of fertilizers can be explained
in the science classes, and their use and limitations experienced by the pupils as they see them in use. The possibilities of proper grazing practices, and of terracing and
soil conservation methods can all be taught theoretically,
at the same time as they are put into practice; the students
will then understand what they are doing and why, and will
be able to analyse any failures and consider possibilities
for greater improvement.

But the school farms must not be, and indeed could not
be, highly mechanized demonstration farms. We do not
have the capital which would be necessary for this to happen,
and neither would it teach the pupils anything about the
life they will be leading. The school farms must be created
by the school community clearing their own bush, and so
on—but doing it together. They must be used with no
more capital assistance than is available to an ordinary,
established, co-operative farm where the work can be
supervised. By such means the students can learn the
advantages of co-operative endeavour, even when outside
capital is not available in any significant quantities. Again,
the advantages of co-operation could be studied in the
classroom, as well as being demonstrated on the farm.

The most important thing is that the school members
should learn that it is their farm, and that their living
standards depend on it. Pupils should be given an opportunity to make many of the decisions necessary—for
example, whether to spend money they have earned on
hiring a tractor to get land ready for planting, or whether

to use that money for other purposes on the farm or in the school, and doing the hard work themselves by sheer physical labour. By this sort of practice and by this combination of classroom work and farm work, our educated young people will learn to realize that if they farm well they can eat well and have better facilities in the dormitories, recreation rooms, and so on. If they work badly, then they themselves will suffer. In this process Government should avoid laying down detailed and rigid rules; each school must have considerable flexibility. Only then can the potential of that particular area be utilized, and only then can the participants practise—and learn to value—direct democracy.

By such means our students will relate work to comfort. They will learn the meaning of living together and working together for the good of all, and also the value of working together with the local non-school community. For they will learn that many things require more than school effort—that irrigation may be possible if they work with neighbouring farmers, that development requires a choice between present and future satisfaction, both for themselves and their village.

At the beginning it is probable that a good number of mistakes will be made, and it would certainly be wrong to give complete untrammelled choice to young pupils right from the start. But although guidance must be given by the school authorities and a certain amount of discipline exerted, the pupils must be able to participate in decisions and learn by mistakes. For example, they can learn to keep a school farm log in which proper records are kept of the work done, the fertilizers applied, or food given to the animals, etc., and the results from different parts of the farm. Then they can be helped to see where changes are required, and why. For it is also important that the idea of planning be taught in the classroom and related to the farm; the whole school should join in the programming of a year's work, and the breakdown of responsibility and timing within that overall programme. Extra benefits to particular groups within the school might then well be related to the proper fulfilment of the tasks set, once all the members of the school have received the necessary minimum for healthy development. Again, this sort of planning can be part of the teaching of socialism.

Where schools are situated in the rural areas, and in relation to new schools built in the future, it should be possible for the school farm to be part of the school site. But in towns, and in some of the old-established schools in heavily populated areas, this will not be possible. In such cases a school might put more emphasis on other productive activities, or it may be that in boarding schools the pupils can spend part of the school year in the classroom and another part in camp on the school farm some distance away. The plan for each school will have to be worked out; it would certainly be wrong to exclude urban schools, even when they are day schools, from this new approach.

Many other activities now undertaken for pupils, especially in secondary schools, should be undertaken by the pupils themselves. After all, a child who starts school at 7 years of age is already 14 before he enters secondary school, and may be 20 or 21 when he leaves. Yet in many of our schools now we employ cleaners and gardeners, not just to supervise and teach but to do all that work. The pupils get used to the idea of having their food prepared by servants, their plates washed up for them, their rooms cleaned, and the school garden kept attractive. If they are asked to participate in these tasks, they even feel aggrieved and do as little as possible, depending on the strictness of the teacher's supervision. This is because they have not learned to take a pride in having clean rooms and nice gardens, in the way that they have learned to take a pride in a good essay or a good mathematics paper. But is it impossible for these tasks to be incorporated into the total teaching task of the school? Is it necessary for head teachers and their secretaries to spend hours working out travel warrants for school holidays, and so on? Can none of these things be incorporated into classroom teaching so that pupils learn how to do these things for themselves by doing them? Is it impossible, in other words, for secondary schools at least to become reasonably self-sufficient communities, where the teaching and supervisory skills are imported from outside, but where other tasks are either done by the community or paid for by its productive efforts? It is true that, to the pupils, the school is only a temporary community, but for up to seven years this is the group to which they really belong.

Obviously such a position could not be reached overnight. It requires a basic change in both organization and teaching, and will therefore have to be introduced gradually, with the schools taking an increasing responsibility for their own well-being as the months pass. Neither would primary schools be able to do as much for themselves—although it should be remembered that the older pupils will be 13 and 14 years of age, at which time children in many European countries are already at work.

But, although primary schools cannot accept the same responsibility for their own well-being as secondary schools, it is absolutely vital that they, and their pupils, should be thoroughly integrated into the village life. The pupils must remain an integral part of the family (or community) economic unit. The children must be made part of the community by having responsibilities to the community, and having the community involved in school activities. The school work—terms, times, and so on—must be so

arranged that the children can participate, as members
of the family, in the family farms, or as junior members of
the community on community farms. At present children
who do not go to school work on the family or community
farm, or look after cattle, as a matter of course. It must
be equally a matter of course that the children who do
attend school should participate in the family work—not
as a favour when they feel like it, but as a normal part of
their upbringing. The present attitudes whereby the school
is regarded as something separate, and the pupils as people
who do not have to contribute to the work, must be abandoned. In this, of course, parents have a special duty;
but the schools can contribute a great deal to the development of this attitude.

There are many different ways in which this integration
can be achieved. But it will have to be done deliberately,
and with the conscious intention of making the children
realize that they are being educated by the community in
order that they shall become intelligent and active members
of the community. One possible way of achieving this
would give to primary school pupils the same advantages of learning by doing as the secondary school pupils
will have. If the primary school children work on a village
communal farm—perhaps having special responsibility for
a given number of acres—they can learn new techniques
and take a pride in a school community achievement. If
there is no communal farm, then the school can start a
small one of their own by appealing to the older members
to help in the bush-clearing in return for a school contribution in labour to some existing community project.

Again, if development work—new buildings or other
things—are needed in the school, then the children and
the local villagers should work on it together, allocating
responsibility according to comparative health and strength.

The children should certainly do their own cleaning (boys as well as girls should be involved in this), and should learn the value of working together and of planning for the future. Thus for example, if they have their own shamba the children should be involved not only in the work, but also in the allocation of any food or cash crop produced. They should participate in the choice between benefit to the school directly, or to the village as a whole, and between present or future benefit. By these and other appropriate means the children must learn from the beginning to the end of their school life that education does not set them apart, but is designed to help them be effective members of the community—for their own benefit as well as that of their country and their neighbours.

One difficulty in the way of this kind of reorganization is the present examination system; if pupils spend more of their time on learning to do practical work, and on contributing to their own upkeep and the development of the community, they will not be able to take the present kind of examinations—at least within the same time period. It is, however, difficult to see why the present examination system should be regarded as sacrosanct. Other countries are moving away from this method of selection, and either abandoning examinations altogether at the lowest levels, or combining them with other assessments. There is no reason why Tanzania should not combine an examination, which is based on the things we teach, with a teacher and pupil assessment of work done for the school and community. This would be a more appropriate method of selecting entrants for secondary schools and for university, teacher training colleges, and so on, than the present purely academic procedure. Once a more detailed outline of this new approach to education is worked out, the question of selection procedure should be looked at again.

This new form of working in our schools will require some considerable organizational change. It may be also that the present division of the school year into rigid terms with long holidays would have to be re-examined; animals cannot be left alone for part of the year, nor can a school farm support the students if everyone is on holiday when the crops need planting, weeding or harvesting. But it should not be impossible for school holidays to be staggered so that different forms go at different periods or, in double-stream secondary schools, for part of a form to go at one time and the rest at another. It would take a considerable amount of organization and administration, but there is no reason why it could not be done if we once make up our minds to it.

It will probably be suggested that if the children are working as well as learning they will therefore be able to learn less academically, and that this will affect standards of administration, in the professions and so on, throughout our nation in time to come. In fact it is doubtful whether this is necessarily so; the recent tendency to admit children to primary schools at ages of 5 and 6 years has almost certainly meant that less can be taught at the early stages. The reversion to 7 or 8 years entrance will allow the pace to be increased somewhat; the older children inevitably learn a little faster. A child is unlikely to learn less academically if his studies are related to the life he sees around him.

But even if this suggestion were based on provable fact, it could not be allowed to over-ride the need for change in the direction of educational integration with our national life. For the majority of our people the thing which matters is that they should be able to read and write fluently in Swahili, that they should have an ability to do arithmetic, and that they should know something of the history, values, and workings of their country and their Government, and that they should acquire the skills necessary to earn their living. (It is important to stress that in Tanzania most people will earn their living by working on their own or on a communal shamba, and only a few will do so by working for wages which they have to spend on buying things the farmer produces for himself.) Things like health science, geography, and the beginning of English, are also important, especially so that the people who wish may be able to learn more by themselves in later life. But most important of all is that our primary school graduates should be able to fit into, and to serve, the communities from which they come.

The same principles of integration into the community, and applicability to its needs, must also be followed at post-secondary levels, but young people who have been through such an integrated system of education as that outlined are unlikely to forget their debt to the community by an intense period of study at the end of their formal educational life. Yet even at university, medical school, or other post-secondary levels, there is no reason why students should continue to have all their washing up and cleaning done for them. Nor is there any reason why students at such institutions should not be required as part of their degree or professional training, to spend at least part of their vacations contributing to the society in a manner related to their studies. At present some undergraduates spend their vacations working in Government offices—getting paid at normal employee rates for doing so. It would be more appropriate (once the organization had been set up efficiently) for them to undertake projects needed by the community, even if there is insufficient money for them to constitute paid employment. For example, the collection of local history, work on the census, participation in adult education activities, work in dispensaries, etc., would give the students practical experience in their own fields. For this they could receive the equivalent of the minimum wage, and any balance of money due for work which would otherwise have been done for higher wages could be paid to the college or institution and go towards welfare or sports equipment. Such work should earn credits for the student which count towards his examination result; a student who shirks such work—or fails to do it properly—would then find that two things follow. First, his fellow students might be blaming him for shortfalls in proposed welfare or other improvements; and second, his degree would be down-graded accordingly.

## Conclusion

The education provided by Tanzania for the students of Tanzania must serve the purposes of Tanzania. It must encourage the growth of the socialist values we aspire to. It must encourage the development of a proud, independent and free citizenry which relies upon itself for its own development, and which knows the advantages and the problems of co-operation. It must ensure that the educated know themselves to be an integral part of the nation and recognize the responsibility to give greater service the greater the opportunities they have had.

This is not only a matter of school organization and curriculum. Social values are formed by family, school, and society—by the total environment in which a child develops. But it is no use our educational system stressing values and knowledge appropriate to the past or to the citizens in other countries; it is wrong if it even contributes to the continuation of those inequalities and privileges which still exist in our society because of our inheritance.

Let our students be educated to be members and servants of the kind of just and egalitarian future to which this country aspires.

# 5

# The Varied Paths to Socialism

*Address to Cairo University, 10 April 1967*

The United Arab Republic and Tanzania are both committed to building socialism, and I would like to use the opportunity of your kind invitation to reflect upon what this means. In particular I wish to direct my remarks to considering its implications for those of us who are—or who may be in the future—in positions of authority or responsibility.

Over time there have been many definitions of socialism, and many books have been written which purport to explain its requirements and implications. Some of these have been valuable analyses of the problems in general, or of problems existing in particular places. We can learn from these writings.

Unfortunately, however, there has grown up what I can only call a 'theology of socialism'. People argue—sometimes quite violently—about what is the true doctrine, or what this or that writer meant when he used a particular phrase. This would not matter if it were simply a recreation of intellectuals, but in fact we have the peculiar position where leaders grappling with existing problems are denounced, or approved, on the grounds that they are—or are not —'acting in accordance with the book'—or one person's interpretation of the book.

## No Man is Infallible
Frankly this seems to me to be absurd. I am a Christian

and it is part of my belief that the word of God is expressed in the Bible. To me, therefore, in spite of—or even because of—the contradictions of the Bible, it is quite sensible to try to get its full meaning, and, when I am trying to act in accordance with God's wishes, to refer to those who have given the Bible a detailed study. I believe that the same thing is true of those who accept the Koran as the inspired word of God's Prophet Mohammed. But the books on socialism are different. They are written by men; wise and clever men perhaps—but still men. Consequently we should use their books as we use the work of living people—knowing that one individual may contribute greatly to the solution of a problem, but that no man is infallible. Indeed, I think that this idea that there is one 'pure socialism', for which the recipe is already known, is an insult to human intelligence. It seems to me that man has yet to solve the problem of living in society, and that each of us may have something to contribute to the problems it involves. We should recognize that there are books on socialism which can illuminate the problems, and books which chart a way forward from a particular point. But that is all.

It is imperative that socialists continue thinking. And this thinking must be more than an attempt to discover what any so-called socialist Bible or socialist Koran really says and means. It is necessary that those who call themselves scientific socialists should be scientific! In that case they would accept or reject socialist ideas and methods in accordance with the objective circumstances of time and place. They would certainly not be hampered or inhibited by the irrelevancies of a socialist theology.

Let me hasten to add that, in conformity with this approach to socialism, I consider that my remarks here today are simply a contribution to the continuing discussion—no more!

Yet I am not saying that, in my view, socialism is a vague concept which can have as many different meanings and variations as there are people who advocate it. A useful definition of the basic assumption and purposes of socialism is not only possible; it is also essential. And from that basis certain practical principles do inevitably follow. But principles become effective only when they are applied to situations. To say that human life is sacred is to state a principle, but that principle only becomes meaningful when it is applied to saving someone from danger or refraining from such action as might jeopardize someone else's well-being. The principle is essential to social living; but it does not give an answer to every life situation—for example, what should be done when a psychotic murderer's life threatens the safety of other people.

## The Basic Purpose of Socialism

For socialism the basic purpose is the well-being of the people, and the basic assumption is an acceptance of human equality. For socialism there must be a belief that every individual man and woman, whatever colour, shape, race, creed, religion, or sex, is an equal member of society, with equal rights in the society and equal duties to it.

A person who does not accept this may accept many policies pursued by socialists; but he cannot be a socialist. Nor can any social organization which is based on inequality justify the support of socialists, whatever its political or economic practices. The so-called 'national socialists' of Nazi Germany were no more socialist than the racialist government of South Africa is socialist—any particular policies of government control of the economy notwithstanding. In socialism there is no room for racialism, and no room either for doctrines of aristocracy. Neither is there any room for that kind of arrogance which leads educated men and women to despise the uneducated. The human equality before God which is the basis of all the great religions of the world is also the basis of the political philosophy of socialism.

Yet socialism is not Utopian. Nor is it unaware that men are unequal in their capacities. On the contrary it is based on the facts of human nature. It is a doctrine which accepts mankind as it is, and demands such an organization of society that man's inequalities are put to the service of his equality.

Socialism is, in fact, the application of the principle of human equality to the social, economic, and political organization of society. It is a recognition that some human beings are physically strong and others weak, that some are intellectually able while others are rather dull, that some people are skilful in the use of their hands while others are clumsy. It involves, too, a recognition that every person has both a selfish and a social instinct which are often in conflict. Socialist doctrine then demands the deliberate organization of society in such a manner that it is impossible—or at least very difficult—for individual desires to be pursued at the cost of other people, or for individual strength to be used for the exploitation of others.

For a socialist state these requirements have both a negative and a positive aspect. Men must be prevented from exploiting each other. And at the same time institutions and organization must be such that man's needs and progress can be co-operatively secured.

## Socialism is against Exploitation and Injustice

There are two paths through which exploitation has been historically secured, and which must therefore be blocked. The first was the use of naked force. Originally through

physical strength, and then through a monopoly of weapons of force, men imposed their will upon others. Armies
were the instruments by which a minority kept an exploited
majority under submission. The kind of revolution which
took place in Egypt, where an army converted itself
from being an instrument of oppression into being an
instrument of the people in opposing oppression, is rare
indeed. More usually it is the gradual growth of law,
and the principle of equality before the law, which ease
the severity of oppression until the people are in a position
to take control of their own destiny.

But equality in law—even the theory of equality in the
making of law—is not sufficient by itself. For the fact
is that equality is indivisible. In practice it is not possible
to be equal in some respects but not in others. Thus it is
that in aristocratic societies a 'noble' and a 'commoner' are
not equal before the law. It will be very unusual for the
latter to defeat the former when they go to law for justice,
and rare too for each to receive equal treatment for comparable offences against the society. Similarly, a rich man and
a poor man are not equally treated for offences, nor equally
likely to receive justice from the society in cases of dispute.

The Rule of Law, and Equality before the Law, are one
essential means of preventing exploitation. But they are only
practical when the society as a whole is based on the
principles of equality—when, in other words, a socialist
policy is being followed. Human beings being fallible,
socialism does not guarantee justice; it has to be worked
for and maintained even in a socialist society. But it is
certain that it cannot be truly achieved except in that
context.

The second major means of exploitation has been
through private property. For when one man controls
the means by which another earns or obtains the food,

clothing, and shelter which are essential to life, then there is no equality. One man must call another 'master'—for he is the master of life as truly as if he had the power to kill with a gun. The man whose means of living are controlled by another, must serve the interests of this other regardless of his own desires or his needs. The nations which experienced feudalism and serfdom know this by experience. But it is as true in capitalist societies where the industries which men depend upon for their wages can be closed, contracted or expanded, and the workers have no voice in the decision and no alternative way of obtaining their food.

If a society is to be made up of equal citizens, then each man must control his own means of production. The farmer must own his own tools—his hoe or his plough. The carpenter must have his own saw and not be dependent upon the whims of another for its use. And so on. The tools of production must be under the control of the individual or group which depends upon them for life.

In African traditional life this was the normal routine. In only a few small areas of Tanzania, for example, was there anything approaching a feudal system. Over the greater part of the country each family worked the land it had cleared, with its own tools, and for its own benefit. But there can be no going back to this system—which has now suffered considerably from the effects of a money economy. It was effective only at a primitive level of life, and left people prey to the vagaries of the weather and subject to other natural calamities.

### Group or Communal Ownership

To secure a good life it is necessary to take advantage of at least some of the modern knowledge and modern techniques. Thus, individual ownership of the tools of

production is no longer universally possible; our people
want the products of mass production and the easier life
which this technology makes possible. Even in agriculture
we can no longer rest content with the situation where
each farmer owns his own jembe and panga, and uses them
as his only tools. By such methods the farmers sweat for
very little result. Yet as soon as the more efficient and
complicated tools are used, individual ownership becomes
either impossible or a great waste of resources. For example, even if it were possible to provide each family in our
wheat producing areas with a combine harvester, it would
be absurd to do so. If the scale of operations were such
that this machine could be economically used, then one
family could not by themselves undertake all the other
operations which would be involved. The family would
have to employ labour to do these other things—and so
we would again be in a situation of exploitation, where one
man's livelihood depends upon the decisions of another.

In those areas of production where individual ownership
of tools is impractical we are therefore forced to the conclusion that group ownership of the means of production
is the only way in which the exploitation of man by man
can be prevented. This communal ownership can be
through the state, which represents every citizen, or through
some other institution which is controlled by those involved
—such as, for example, a co-operative, or a local authority.

The same thing applies to the question of distribution
and exchange. In small peasant societies it is possible for
each grower or each producer to bring his goods to a
central place and bargain with those who are interested
in acquiring them. But the increasing specialization of
production which is involved in modern methods requires
more sophisticated techniques. And once again, a private
individual can then get into a position where he controls

the well-being of another. He can do this by his charges
for transport, by his commission on sales, or by exploiting
a monopoly position which is economically justified.

Communal ownership of the means of distribution—
the railways, or the lorries, etc.—and communal enterprise
in the act of bargaining, can eliminate this kind of exploitation. At the same time communal ownership in both
production and distribution can provide the machinery
through which new initiatives for public well-being can
be undertaken. For example, a group of farmers together can
raise the capital and get access to the technical know-how
which is necessary to control a stream and put it to service.
Or the residents in an area can together build a road or a
bridge, knowing that it will be for mutual benefit. They
will not fear that it might just benefit the individual who
happens to have a lorry—and who may not reduce his
charges although his vehicle no longer suffers damage from
fording a stream, and so on.

Yet although the facts of modern technology provide the
final justification for the communal ownership of the means
of production and exchange, it is not always and everywhere
appropriate. The principle of social ownership and control
does not provide a detailed answer to every problem. It is
possible, as we have found out in Tanzania, for farmers to
be exploited even by their own co-operative and their own
state if the machinery is not correct, or if the managers
and workers are inefficient or dishonest. And it is possible
for group ownership to result in a stultification of development, and such stagnation that in the end the producers
would get greater benefit from controlled forms of individual
exploitation. For it is not good enough just to deprive
people of the incentives of selfishness. Development requires that these should be replaced by effective social
incentives. While these do not exist, or to the extent that

they do not exist, we have seriously to consider whether, and how far, we can dispense with the incentives of private profit at that time.

### The Purpose of Socialist Organization must be the Central Factor

So we get problems of what can be and should be socially owned or controlled at each stage in a society's development. Even of things which are quite basic to a nation's economy, public ownership may not necessarily and always be the correct answer for socialists at a particular time. Especially where public ownership means disruption of an existing industry, alternative methods of public control may be appropriate. This can sometimes be exercised through other means—through legislation, veto, consultation, and so on. A decision should depend on the circumstances and the prevailing attitudes—that is, on the success of socialist political education. We have to accept, however, that anything short of ownership often requires a sophisticated and expensive administrative structure if it is not to be simply negative in its effects. In making all such decisions the purpose of socialist organization must be the central factor. That purpose is the service of the people. You do not often serve the people by actions which outrage their feelings, even if those actions are intended to give them collective control over a vital element of their livelihood.

Take, for example, the question of land. In Tanzania we abolished freehold ownership of land shortly after independence. All land now belongs to the nation. But this was not an affront to our people; communal ownership of land is traditional in our country—it was the concept of freehold which had been foreign to them. In tribal tradition an individual or family secured rights in land for as long as they were using it. It became the family land when it was cleared and planted; for the rest of the time it was tribal land, and it reverted to tribal land if the family stopped working it. The only change which our law effected as far as the masses were concerned was that the land became national instead of tribal—and we have been fortunate enough in Tanzania for this transition to be an easy one. Thus only about 1 per cent of our land was really affected by this law, and no Tanzanian who really wants to farm has been unable to find the necessary land—even if not just where he wants it.

These circumstances have meant that the land reforms which were an essential ingredient of the revolution in Egypt would be inapplicable to Tanzania. Equally, our modified traditional ownership system may be quite irrelevant here, or at least quite inappropriate. But the purpose of our different moves has in both cases been socialistic. Both of our states have acted to secure the use of land for the service of the people, and to prevent it providing a basis for inescapable exploitation.

Yet for neither of our countries is the present action the end of all action. Having secured or controlled ownership, we have to decide what is done with the land, and how it is done. And then we have to implement those decisions. This means down-to-earth, village-level decisions which are acceptable to the people there, and at the same time compatible with the larger aims and interests of the society as a whole. And if the correct socialist policy on ownership between two socialist states is different, surely the correct decisions at this lower level will also be different. Indeed, differences may exist at this level even within the one state according to the experiences of the people in a particular place, and the geophysical circumstances existing in that locality.

Of course it is not only in relation to land and agriculture that a socialist policy will vary between different countries. We in Tanzania have recently engaged in a small nationalization exercise, and in other cases have secured majority control in private enterprises. We are now in the stage where people are debating whether we acted correctly or not. Some people criticize us for outright nationalization; some for not nationalizing all industry and commerce; and still other groups criticize us for using former owners as managers of publicly owned industries and businesses. Needless to say, there are other groups which applaud those same actions. We welcome such discussion when it is constructively based on the needs of Tanzania. Out of such discussion what may not have been clear before becomes clear, and rationality continually guides us on our socialist path.

But despite their importance for the future, and despite the attention that our recent public ownership measures have attracted internationally, they are only a small part of the real task Tanzania has now undertaken. In our case agricultural development—and therefore a socialist agricultural policy—is the central issue, and the core of Tanzania's development of self-reliant socialism. And this we have hardly begun. But we have land in abundance, and traditional agricultural methods which fail to make full use either of the land itself or of the energies of our people. It appears to me that these facts will inevitably cause differences of emphasis and organization between the socialist policies of Tanzania and those of the United Arab Republic. For here, as I understand it, you have the problems of a rapidly rising population pressing heavily upon arable land resources, and agricultural methods already to some extent adapted to the needs of intensive agriculture. These are different problems from ours, and your measures to bring socialism may therefore be different too. And surely, if such different policies are needed between our two parts of the African continent—linked as they are by the Nile waters—even greater differences will be correct socialist policy between either of us and nations elsewhere.

## Socialist Policies will vary from Place to Place

It may be that ultimately—when we have created socialist states instead of being engaged in building them—the institutions and organization in all socialist countries will be very similar. I do not know. The evidence does not yet exist. But I am convinced that the paths to the point where our respective peoples control their own livelihood and their own development will certainly be different. A man coming to Cairo from Dar es Salaam goes in the opposite direction from that taken by a man coming to Cairo from Moscow. What matters is that each should go in the correct direction from his particular departure point!

It is not possible for a country which moves to socialism from a highly developed capitalist economy, to follow the same path as one which starts from a backward peasant economy. Nor is it likely that two backward countries moving to socialism will follow exactly the same path if one starts from a feudal base and another from traditional communalism. Each state must move in a direction which is appropriate to its starting point.

Although, however, each country with a socialist purpose has a different path to tread, we can still learn a great deal from each other. Indeed I believe that we can even learn from other countries which are not avowedly socialist, but which are tackling similar problems of development. The transformation of our people's lives, as a deliberate government policy, is a new development in the history of man. We have very little positive experience to guide us; we must grope our way forward. Undoubtedly we shall make some mistakes in our enthusiasm—or in our caution. Sometimes we shall try things before we are ready; sometimes we shall fail to choose the best methods out of alternatives available to us. And sometimes we may miss opportunities for advance because we are too cautious.

But while none of us has all the answers, we under-developed countries, in particular, can help each other—especially where we have the same socialist objectives. Some of our problems are similar, but we tackle them at different times and in different ways. Why then should each of us act as if there was no experience at all? This would be to display a nationalistic chauvinism which has nothing at all to do with socialism and its belief in the oneness of man. The opportunities for mutual co-operation, and for learning from each other, are endless. Certainly we in Tanzania believe that we can benefit from the longer experience in the UAR. We shall not simply adopt things we see here, but it appears very likely that we shall find ideas and experiences which we can adapt to our own circumstances. It may be that despite our later start, Tanzania too has something it can offer to other socialist countries. That is for others to say! Certainly we shall be willing to make our exper-ience available, if and when it is wanted. But in any case, we hope to learn from what we see here.

Let me conclude these remarks by coming back to my starting point. For although I have been stressing the fact that there is no one single road to socialism, I hope I have also made clear our conviction that there are certain things which are basic to it. And it is these things which are of vital importance to leadership, and to the work of the more highly educated groups of our peoples.

*Socialism cannot be imposed on People*
In 1962 I said that socialism is an attitude of mind.

I still believe this to be true. It does not mean that institutions and organizations are irrelevant. It means that without the correct attitudes institutions can be subverted from their true purpose. First and foremost, there must be this acceptance of human equality. Then there must be, among the leadership, a desire and a determination to serve alongside of, and in complete identification with, the masses. The people must be, and must know themselves to be, sovereign. Socialism cannot be imposed upon people; they can be guided; they can be led. But ultimately they must be involved.

If the people are not involved in public ownership, and cannot control the policies followed, the public ownership can lead to fascism, not socialism. If the people are not sovereign, then they can suffer under dreadful tyranny imposed in their name. If the people are not honestly served by those to whom they have entrusted responsibility, then corruption can negate all their efforts and make them abandon their socialist ideas.

The political institutions and organizations through which the people's sovereignty is expressed will vary from one state to another, and one time to another, just as the economic institutions of socialism vary. The means most appropriate will depend upon many historical and geographical factors. But ultimately socialism is only possible if the people as a whole are involved in the government of their political and economic affairs. Their efforts must be mobilized. Sometimes this will mean going more slowly, sometimes faster, than academic considerations alone would determine. But the involvement of the people is vital, for socialism is nothing if it is not of the people.

This is a technological age, and many decisions cannot be taken directly by the masses. Tremendous responsibilities therefore rest upon those of us who have had the privilege of higher education. We have been educated out of the resources of the people. Now we have, on their behalf, to deal with complex administrative and technical matters and to make choices which affect their welfare. We have the responsibility to give advice to the people on issues where the implications may not be clear. All these things we must do to the best of our ability. But we must recognize, too, that our function is to serve, to guide the masses through the complexities of modern technology—to propose, to explain, and to persuade. For our education does not give us rights over the people. It does not justify arrogance, nor attitudes of superiority.

The only justification for bureaucracies, for industries—or for universities—is the greater well-being of the human beings who constitute the society. And unless we who have power—whether it be political or technical—remain at one with the masses, then we cannot serve them. Our opportunity is unparalleled in man's history. We must meet the challenge with courage, and with humility.

# 6

# The Purpose is Man

*A speech at Dar es Salaam University College,
5 August 1967*

---

The Arusha Declaration is a declaration of intent; no more than that. It states the goal towards which TANU will be leading the people of Tanzania, and it indicates the direction of development. Neither on 5th February, nor on any day since, has Tanzania suddenly become a socialist state, a self-reliant state, or a developed state.

The Arusha Declaration could not achieve these things, and nor would it have been possible for any amount of enthusiasm and energy in implementation to have achieved them in the months since it was adopted by our Party. The Declaration is the beginning, not the end, of a very long and probably extremely hard struggle.

It is necessary that we should be very clear about these things, for otherwise we shall fail to reach the goal stated and shall be liable to do great damage to our nation. We must understand fully what the Arusha Declaration is, what it says, and what it implies for the near as well as the distant future.

*We shall remain Tanzanians*

The Declaration is first of all a reaffirmation of the fact that we are Tanzanians and wish to remain Tanzanian as we develop. Certainly we shall wish to change very many things in our present society. But we have stated that these changes will be effected through the processes of growth in certain directions. This growth must come out of our own roots, not through the grafting on to those roots of something which is alien to our society. This is very important, for it means that we cannot adopt any political 'holy book' and try to implement its rulings—with or without revision.

It means that our social change will be determined by our own needs as we see them, and in the direction that we feel to be appropriate for us at any particular time. We shall draw sustenance from universal human ideas and from the practical experiences of other peoples; but we start from a full acceptance of our African-ness and a belief that in our own past there is very much which is useful for our future.

## Commitment to a Quality of Life

The Arusha Declaration is also a commitment to a particular quality of life. It is based on the assumption of human equality, on the belief that it is wrong for one man to dominate or to exploit another, and on the knowledge that every individual hopes to live in society as a free man able to lead a decent life in conditions of peace with his neighbours. The document is, in other words, man-centred.

Inherent in the Arusha Declaration, therefore, is a rejection of the concept of national grandeur as distinct from the well-being of its citizens, and a rejection too of material wealth for its own sake. It is a commitment to the belief that there are more important things in life than the amassing of riches, and that if the pursuit of wealth clashes with things like human dignity and social equality, then the latter will be given priority.

For in a Tanzania which is implementing the Arusha Declaration, the purpose of all social, economic and political activity must be man—the citizens, and all the citizens, of this country. The creation of wealth is a good thing and something which we shall have to increase. But it will cease to be good the moment wealth ceases to serve man and begins to be served by man.

## Freedom must be maintained

With our present level of economic activity, and our present poverty, this may seem to be an academic point; but in reality it is very fundamental. For it means that there are certain things which we shall refuse to do or to accept, either as individuals or as a nation, even if the result of them would be a surge forward in our economic development.

For example, even if it were true—which I do not believe—that we could achieve a very great increase in the statistical national wealth and in the income of the majority of our people, we would still reject a proposal that a single foreign country or a group of individuals should establish a complex of agricultural estates, heavy and light industries, etc.

We would reject such a proposal because of its effect upon our national independence, and because large numbers of our people would become the paid servants of another nation or another person. The destiny and the whole life of the people of Tanzania would, in such a case, be controlled by another country or by a few individuals. Either of these things would be inconsistent with our commitment to Tanzanian freedom and to the freedom and human equality of all citizens.

## Progress by Evolution

Yet this does not mean that we have in any way accepted our present poverty. On the contrary, the Arusha Declaration calls for a tremendous human effort for change. We are saying that what has taken the older countries centuries should take us decades. What we are attempting is a telescoped evolution of our economy and of our society. This is not a sociological, or even a biological, impossibility.

It has taken hundreds of millions of years for life on the earth to develop from simple living matter to the complicated and inter-linked cell structure which is a human being. Yet a human foetus develops from one to the other in nine months.

The national growth of our country can be telescoped and yet remain organic. It will take more than nine months; but the union of our people and our land, in the light of the human knowledge available in this century, can certainly shorten very considerably the period during which countries like the United Kingdom or the United States achieved their present affluence.

## *Integrated Programme based on Linked Principles*

The other important fact about the Arusha Declaration is that it is an integrated programme of action based on linked principles. There are some people who would like to support the call for national self-reliance, but have strong reservations about the socialist doctrines and especially the leadership qualifications.

There are others who claim to support the socialist aspects but have reservations about the statement that Tanzania must depend upon its own resources for development and act accordingly. There are still other people who have tried (usually with ulterior motives) to interpret it as an anti-Asian, or anti-European, document; or who criticize it on the grounds that it supports the interests of these groups against the interests of black people in Tanzania. But the truth is that it is not possible to accept socialism without self-reliance, or vice versa; and it is not possible to talk racialism while still claiming to accept the Arusha Declaration.

Self-reliance in development is merely an application of something we knew in 1954—that only Tanzanians are sufficiently interested to develop Tanzania in the interests of Tanzanians, and only Tanzanians can say what those interests are. And socialism is an application to economic and social life of the doctrine of human equality which we appealed to when we rejected the right of any other nation to govern us.

These two things are but different sides of the single coin —human equality. And most clearly of all, the Arusha Declaration refers to men, and to systems—not to members of particular racial or tribal groups. The person who claims to use it in support of attacks on any particular racial community, is betraying both his ignorance and his rejection of the principles enunciated in it.

### The Implications of Self-Reliance

What, then, is the meaning of self-reliance, and what are its implications for our future policies? First and foremost, it means that for our development we have to depend upon ourselves and our own resources. These resources are land, and people. Certainly we have a few factories, we have a small diamond mine, and so on. But it is important to realize that (when measured in 1960 prices) out of a gross domestic product estimated at Shs. 4,646/- million in 1966, some Shs. 2,669/- million—that is, more than 57 per cent— was the direct result of agricultural activities. Only Shs. 321/- million was the combined result of mining and manufacturing; that is to say that all the mining and manufacturing of Tanzania produced last year less than 7 per cent of the gross domestic product.

The one thing we certainly do not have is money searching for investment opportunities. The *per capita* income, in terms of 1966 prices, was about Shs. 525/- last year. That does not allow very much to be withdrawn from current consumption and invested in development. Indeed, we did very well last year to find Shs. 135/- million (that is, about Shs. 14/- per person) from internal resources for development.

But to provide one job in a highly mechanized industry can cost Shs. 40,000/- or more. To build the oil refinery cost more than Shs. 110/- million. To build a modern steel mill would cost rather more than that.

### Development through Agriculture

On the other hand, it is possible to double the output of cotton on a particular acre by spending Shs. 130/- on fertilizer and insecticide; it is possible to double a farmer's acreage under crops by the provision of an ox-plough at a cost of Shs. 250/- or less, and so on. In other words, whereas it is possible to find the sort of investment capital which can bring great increases in agricultural output from our present resources, it is not possible for us to envisage establishing heavy industries, or even very much in the way of light industries, in the near future.

To be realistic, therefore, we must stop dreaming of developing Tanzania through the establishment of large, modern industries. For such things we have neither the money nor the skilled manpower required to make them efficient and economic. We would even be making a mistake if we think in terms of covering Tanzania with mechanized farms, using tractors and combine harvesters.

Once again, we have neither the money nor the skilled manpower, nor in this case the social organization which could make such investment possible and economic. This is not to say that there will be no new modern industries and no mechanized farms. But they will be the exception, not

the rule, and they will be entered upon to meet particular
problems. They are not the answer to the basic development
needs of Tanzania.

## And Appropriate Agricultural Methods

This is what the Arusha Declaration makes clear in
both economic and social terms. Our future lies in the development of our agriculture, and in the development of our
rural areas. But because we are seeking to grow from our
own roots and to preserve that which is valuable in our
traditional past, we have also to stop thinking in terms of
massive agricultural mechanization and the proletarianiza-
tion of our rural population.

We have, instead, to think in terms of development
through the improvement of the tools we now use, and
through the growth of co-operative systems of production.
Instead of aiming at large farms using tractors and other
modern equipment and employing agricultural labourers,
we should be aiming at having ox-ploughs all over
the country.

The jembe will have to be eliminated by the ox-plough
before the latter can be eliminated by the tractor. We cannot
hope to eliminate the jembe by the tractor. Instead of thinking about providing each farmer with his own lorry, we
should consider the usefulness of oxen-drawn carts, which
could be made within the country and which are appropriate
both to our roads and to the loads which each farmer is
likely to have.

Instead of the aerial spraying of crops with insecticide,
we should use hand-operated pumps, and so on. In other
words, we have to think in terms of what is available, or can
be made available, at comparatively small cost, and which
can be operated by the people. By moving into the future

along this path, we can avoid massive social disruption and human suffering.

### Small Industries

At the same time we can develop small industries and service stations in the rural areas where the people live, and thus help to diversify the rural economy. By this method we can achieve a widespread increase in the general level of people's income, instead of concentrating any economic improvement in the hands of a few people. Such capital as we do have will make the widest possible impact by being invested in fertilizers, in credit for better breeding stock, in improved instruments of production, and other similar things. These, although small in themselves, can bring a great proportionate increase in the farmers' incomes.

This does not mean that there will be no new investment in towns, or that there will be no new factories. When you have large numbers of people living together, certain public services are essential for public health and security reasons. It would be absurd to pretend that we can forget the towns, which are in any case often a service centre for the surrounding rural areas.

### Factory Sites

Factories which serve the whole country also have to be sited in places which are convenient for transport and communications. For example, if we had put the Friendship Textile Mill in a rural area, we would have had to invest in special road building, etc. for it to be of any use, and in any case the number of its workers would soon mean that a new town had grown up in that place.

But even when we are building factories which serve the whole nation, we have to consider whether it is necessary for us to use the most modern machinery which exists in the world. We have to consider whether some older equipment which demands more labour, but labour which is less highly skilled, is not better suited to our needs, as well as being more within our capacity to build and use.

## Trade with Others

There are, however, two respects in which our call for self-reliance has been widely misunderstood or deliberately misinterpreted. The doctrine of self-reliance does not imply isolationism, either politically or economically. It means that we shall depend on ourselves, not on others.

But this is not the same thing as saying we shall not trade with other people or co-operate with them when it is to mutual benefit. Obviously we shall do so. We shall have to continue to sell enough of our goods abroad to pay for the things we have to acquire. Up to now Tanzania has always done this; indeed, we have had a surplus of our balance of payments for many years. But the things we sell are the products of our agriculture, and this is likely to continue to be the case despite the problem of commodity prices in the world.

The things we import will increasingly have to be the things which are essential for our development, and which we cannot produce ourselves. Up to now we have been importing many things which a little effort would enable us to provide for ourselves, such as food, as well as luxury items which simply arouse desires among our people which could never be satisfied for more than a tiny minority.

Self-reliance, in other words, is unlikely to reduce our participation in international trade, but it should, over time, change its character to some extent. We should be exporting commodities after at least some preliminary processing, and we should be importing the things which we cannot produce and which are necessary for the development and the welfare of our whole people.

*Tanzania wants Capital Assistance*

The other thing which is necessary to understand about
self-reliance is that Tanzania has not said it does not want
international assistance in its development. We shall
continue to seek capital from abroad for particular projects
or as a contribution to general development. It is clear,
for example, that if we are to achieve our ambition of
getting a railway which links Tanzania and Zambia, we
shall have to obtain most of the capital and the technical
skill from overseas

Overseas capital will also be welcome for any project
where it can make our own efforts more effective—where it
acts as a catalyst for Tanzanian activity. It is for this reason
that the Government has made it clear that we shall welcome outside participation—whether private or government—in the establishment of many different kinds of factories, especially those which produce consumption goods
or process our crops and raw materials.

Capital assistance for education of all kinds is another
of the many fields in which outside assistance can be valuable
provided it is linked to our capacity to meet the recurrent
costs. The important thing, however, is that we in Tanzania
should not adopt an attitude that nothing can be done until
someone else agrees to give us money.

There are many things we can do by ourselves, and we
must plan to do them. There are other things which can
become easier if we get assistance, but these we should
reckon on doing the hard way, by ourselves, only being
thankful if assistance is forthcoming.

*Skilled People are also needed*

But it is not only capital which we must welcome from
outside; it is also men. Few things make me more angry
than a refusal to accept and to work with people from other

countries whose participation can make all the difference between our plans succeeding or failing. It is not being self-reliant to refuse to carry out the directions of a foreign engineer, or a foreign doctor, or a foreign manager; it is just being stupid. It is absolutely vital that Tanzanians should determine policy; but if the implementation of a particular policy requires someone with good educational qualifications or long experience, it is not very sensible to allow that policy to fail through pride.

We must look at this question of employing expatriates scientifically and without prejudice; we must assess the interests of our development as a whole, not the interests of a particular person who feels that he would like the high post concerned but is neither ready for it nor prepared to go on learning from someone else.

## No False Pride in this Matter

Let us take note of the fact that the developed countries have no false pride in this matter. Western Europe and North America recruit trained people from countries like India and Pakistan, and West European countries complain bitterly about what they call the 'brain drain' caused by the richer United States offering high incomes to educated and skilled people.

It has been alleged that the United States has saved itself billions of dollars by attracting workers on whose education it has not spent one cent. Yet while wealthy and developed countries adopt this kind of attitude, we in Tanzania appear to rejoice when we lose a trained person to Europe or North America.

We rejoice on the grounds that it provides us with an opportunity for Africanization, or for self-reliance! Anyone would think that we have a problem of unemployed experts. It is time that we outgrew this childishness; and we must do so quickly if we intend to tackle this problem of modern development really seriously.

### Socialism

What, then, of socialism—the other aspect of the Arusha Declaration? First, it is important to be clear that nationalization of existing industries and commercial undertakings is only a very small part of the socialism which we have adopted. The important thing for us is the extent to which we succeed in preventing the exploitation of one man by another, and in spreading the concept of working together co-operatively for the common good instead of competitively for individual private gain. And the truth is that our economy is now so underdeveloped that it is in growth that we shall succeed or fail in these things.

The nationalization of the banks, of insurance, and of the few industries affected, was important; but much more important is whether we succeed in expanding our economy without expanding the opportunities and the incentives for human exploitation.

Once again this really means that socialism has to spread in the rural areas where our people live. In this we have an advantage over many other countries, just because of our lack of development. Up to now exploitation in agriculture is very limited; the greater part of our farming is still individual peasant farming, or family farming. But although this is not capitalist, neither is it very efficient or productive in comparison with what it could be.

Indeed, it is true that where people work together in groups—and that is mostly in those restricted sectors of capitalist farming—there is often a greater output per worker and per acre. Our objective must be to develop in such a manner as to ensure that the advantages of modern

knowledge and modern methods are achieved, but without
the spread of capitalism.

*Human Equality—the Essence of Socialism*

Socialism, however, is not simply a matter of methods
of production. They are part of it but not all of it. The
essence of socialism is the practical acceptance of human
equality. That is to say, every man's equal right to a decent
life before any individual has a surplus above his needs; his
equal right to participate in government; and his equal
responsibility to work and contribute to the society to the
limit of his ability.

In Tanzania this means that we must safeguard and
strengthen our democratic procedures: we must get to the
position where every citizen plays an active and direct role
in the government of his local community, at the same time
as he plays a full role in the government of his own country.
It also means that we have to correct the glaring income
differentials which we inherited from colonialism, and
ensure that the international imbalance between the wages
of factory and service workers on the one hand, and of
agricultural workers on the other, is not reproduced within
our own nation. We have, in other words, to ensure that
every person gets a return commensurate with the contribution he makes to the society.

But at the same time we have to make dignified provision for
those whose age or disability prevents them from playing a full
role in the economy. We have also to spread—although it can
only be done gradually—equality of opportunity for all citizens, until every person is able to make the kind of contribution to our needs which is most within his capacity and his
desires. But, most of all, we have to reactivate the philosophy
of co-operation in production and sharing in distribution
which was an essential part of traditional African society.

*Change through Growth*

I started this afternoon by saying that the Arusha Declaration is a statement of intent; I hope I have made clear what is intended and have at least indicated some of the implications of this. As I close, however, I want to stress two things.

The first is that the Arusha Declaration lays down a policy of revolution by evolution; we shall become a socialist, self-reliant society through our growth. We cannot afford the destruction of the economic instruments we now have nor a reduction in our present output. The steps by which we move forward must take account of these things. Our change will, therefore, be effected almost entirely by the emphasis of our new development and by the gradual conversion of existing institutions into others more in accordance with our philosophy.

The other thing is that the Arusha Declaration is a general outline. The policy paper Education for Self-Reliance was an interpretation of its meaning in one field; there will be other papers on other aspects of our development. But the scope for individual initiative within this framework is almost unlimited.

We need people, especially in the rural areas, who accept the underlying doctrines of the Arusha Declaration and who are both willing and able to work with, and to lead, their fellow citizens in the promotion of socialist growth. If we have enough people who are purposeful and dedicated in this manner, we shall succeed.

*The Challenge*

The real question, therefore, is whether each of us is prepared to accept the challenge of building a state in which no man is ashamed of his poverty in the light of another's affluence, and no man has to be ashamed of his affluence in the light of another's poverty. Are we prepared to build a society in which all men can treat with others on terms of complete equality and in a spirit of free co-operation? Every one of us has to give the answer to this; but for young people there is a special responsibility. For educated young people there is a special temptation too, because in a capitalist society they would be the ones most likely to attain privilege at the expense of others.

I believe that the young people of Tanzania, educated and uneducated alike, have accepted this challenge. Carrying it through will not always be easy, nor always in every respect popular. In order to do it, it is necessary that there should be a total understanding and acceptance of the objectives and the philosophy of the Arusha Declaration, so that disappointments can be withstood and personal difficulties overcome.

There has to be a recognition that there is a job to be done which will often be difficult, and often demand the renunciation of personal comfort. It will offer in return the challenge and the satisfaction of contributing to the building of a socialist society for the benefit of our children and grandchildren.

# 7

# Socialism and Rural Development

*Policy booklet published in September 1967*

---

The traditional African family lived according to the basic principles of ujamaa. Its members did this unconsciously, and without any conception of what they were doing in political terms. They lived together and worked together because that was how they understood life, and how they reinforced each other against the difficulties they had to contend with—the uncertainties of weather and sickness, the depredations of wild animals (and sometimes human enemies), and the cycle of life and death. The results of their joint effort were divided unequally between them, but according to well-understood customs. And the division was always on the basis of the fact that every member of the family had to have enough to eat, some simple covering, and a place to sleep, before any of them (even the head of the family) had anything extra. The family members thought of themselves as one, and all their language and behaviour emphasized their unity. The basic goods of life were 'our food', 'our land', 'our cattle'. And identity was established in terms of relationships; mother and father of so-and-so; daughter of so-and-so; wife of such and such a person. They lived together and they worked together; and the result of their joint labour was the property of the family as a whole.

## The Assumptions of Traditional Ujamaa Living

This pattern of living was made possible because of three basic assumptions of traditional life. These assumptions were not questioned, or even thought about; but the whole of society was both based upon them, and designed to uphold them. They permeated the customs, manners and education of the people. And although they were not always honoured by every individual, they were not challenged; rather the individual continued to be judged by them.

The first of these basic assumptions, or principles of life, I have sometimes described as 'love', but that word is so often used to imply a deep personal affection that it can give a false impression. A better word is perhaps 'respect', for it was—and is—really a recognition of mutual involvement in one another, and may or may not involve any affection deeper than that of familiarity. Each member of the family recognized the place and the rights of the other members, and although the rights varied according to sex, age, and even ability and character, there was a minimum below which no one could exist without disgrace to the whole family. Even the most junior wife in a polygamous household had respect due to her; she had a right to her own house and in relation to her husband, and she had full access to the joint products of the family group. There was also due to her, and from her, a family loyalty.

While the first principle of the ujamaa unit related to persons, the second related to property. It was that all the basic goods were held in common, and shared among all members of the unit. There was an acceptance that whatever one person had in the way of basic necessities, they all had; no one could go hungry while others hoarded food, and no one could be denied shelter if others had space to spare. Within the extended family, and even within the tribe, the economic level of one person could

never get too far out of proportion to the economic level
of others. There was not complete equality; some individuals within the family, and some families within the clan
or tribe, could 'own' more than others. But in general
they acquired this through extra efforts of their own, and
the social system was such that in time of need it was
available to all. Further, the inheritance systems were
such that in almost all places death led to the dispersal of,
for example, a large herd of cattle, among a large number
of people. Inequalities existed, but they were tempered
by comparable family or social responsibilities, and they
could never become gross and offensive to the social equality
which was at the basis of the communal life.

Finally, and as a necessary third principle, was the fact
that everyone had an obligation to work. The work done
by different people was different, but no one was exempt.
Every member of the family, and every guest who shared
in the right to eat and have shelter, took it for granted that
he had to join in whatever work had to be done. Only
by the universal acceptance of this principle was the continuation of the other two made possible.

## The Inadequacies of the Traditional System

But although these three principles were at the base of the
traditional practice of ujamaa, the result was not the kind
of life which we really wish to see existing throughout
Tanzania. Quite apart from personal failures to live up to
the ideals and principles of the social system (and traditional Africa was no more composed of unselfish and
hard-working angels than any other part of the world),
there were two basic factors which prevented traditional
society from full flowering.

The first of these was that, although every individual
was joined to his fellows by human respect, there was, in

most parts of Tanzania, an acceptance of one human inequality. Although we try to hide the fact, and despite the exaggeration which our critics have frequently indulged in, it is true that the women in traditional society were regarded as having a place in the community which was not only different, but was also to some extent inferior. It is impossible to deny that the women did, and still do, more than their fair share of the work in the fields and in the homes. By virtue of their sex they suffered from inequalities which had nothing to do with their contribution to the family welfare. Although it is wrong to suggest that they have always been an oppressed group, it is true that within traditional society ill treatment and enforced subservience could be their lot. This is certainly inconsistent with our socialist conception of the equality of all human beings and the right of all to live in such security and freedom as is consistent with equal security and freedom of all others. If we want our country to make full and quick progress now, it is essential that our women live on terms of full equality with their fellow citizens who are men.

The other aspect of traditional life which we have to break away from is its poverty. Certainly there was an attractive degree of economic equality, but it was equality at a low level. The equality is good, but the level can be raised. For there was nothing inherent in the traditional system which caused this poverty; it was the result of two things only. The first was ignorance, and the second was the scale of operations. Both of these can be corrected without affecting the validity and applicability of the three principles of mutual respect, sharing of joint production, and work by all. These principles were, and are, the foundation of human security, of real practical human equality, and of peace between members of a society.

They can also be a basis of economic development if modern
knowledge and modern techniques of production are
used.

## The Objective

This is the objective of socialism in Tanzania. To build
a society in which all members have equal rights and equal
opportunities; in which all can live at peace with their
neighbours without suffering or imposing injustice, being
exploited, or exploiting; and in which all have a gradually
increasing basic level of material welfare before any individual lives in luxury.

To create this kind of nation we must build on the firm
foundations of the three principles of the ujamaa family.
But we must add to these principles the knowledge and the
instruments necessary for the defeat of the poverty which
existed in traditional African society. In other words,
we must add those elements which allow for increased
output per worker, and which make a man's efforts yield
more satisfactions to him. We must take our traditional
system, correct its shortcomings, and adapt to its service
the things we can learn from the technologically developed
societies of other continents.

## Tanzania as it has been developing

In recent years this is not what has been happening.
Our society, our economy, and the dominant ambitions of
our own people are all very different now from what they
were before the colonial era. There has been a general
acceptance of the social attitudes and ideas of our colonial
masters. We have got rid of the foreign government, but
we have not yet rid ourselves of the individualistic social
attitudes which they represented and taught. For it was
from these overseas contacts that we developed the idea
that the way to the comfort and prosperity which everyone

wants is through selfishness and individual advancement. And, of course, under a capitalist type of system it is quite true that for a few individuals great wealth and comfort is possible. In even the poorest societies—that is, those societies where the total wealth produced and available in the community is very low—a few individuals can be very wealthy, if others are even poorer than they need be. If you abandon the idea and the goal of equality, and allow the clever and fortunate to exploit the others, then the glittering prizes of material success will be attractive to all, and the temptations of individualism will be further increased. No one likes to be exploited, but all of us are tempted by opportunities to exploit others.

One important result of developments over the past 40 years has been the growth of urban centres and of wage employment. In fact only about 4 per cent of our people live in towns, and less than 340,000 people work for wages out of a total adult population of not less than 5 million. Unfortunately, the life of these tiny minorities has become a matter of great envy for the majority. Life in the towns has come to represent opportunities for advancement, a chance of excitement, and the provision of social services, none of which is easily available in the rural areas. Most of all, there is an almost universal belief that life in the towns is more comfortable and more secure—that the rewards of work are better in the urban areas and that people in the rural parts of the country are condemned to poverty and insecurity for their whole lives.

But although the goal of individual wealth has been accepted by our people, and despite their belief that this can be attained by wage employment and by life in the towns, the truth is that it is an unrealistic goal, especially in Tanzania. The vast majority even of our town dwellers live extremely poorly, and in most cases they are on the whole worse off, both materially and in the realm of personal satisfaction, than the people in the rural areas could be. An unskilled worker in the towns or on the agricultural estates earns wages which are hardly sufficient to enable a family to eat a proper diet and live in a decent house. Certainly the concentration of population in a small area makes it essential (for public health reasons) that the community should spend money on making clean water available within easy distance of everyone; certainly, too, the concentration of people makes social life easier, and allows educational opportunities for adults to be more easily available and more varied. Yet, on the other hand, the life of children outside school is often extremely bad, unhealthy and dangerous, and for most people the ever-present threat of unemployment, and consequent real hunger in the midst of apparent wealth, introduces evils which can be excluded from life in the rural areas if this is based on the traditional principles of African society.

## Changes in the Rural Areas

Yet it is not only through the growth of towns that our society has changed. Even in the rural areas life has been changing over the past 30 years or so. Self-sufficient family farms producing just their own food with enough over to obtain clothes and pay taxes, are no longer universal. Even where subsistence agriculture is still practised, the young and active men have often left the homestead to go to towns or to seek elsewhere for the modern world.

But the basic difference between Tanzania's rural life now and in the past stems from the widespread introduction of cash crop farming. Over large areas of the country peasants spend at least part of their time—and sometimes the larger part of it—on the cultivation of crops for sale—crops like cotton, coffee, sisal, pyrethrum, and so on. But in the process the old traditions of living together, working together, and sharing the proceeds, have often been abandoned. Farmers tend to work as individuals, in competition and not in co-operation with their neighbours. And in many places our most intelligent and hard-working peasants have invested their money (or money advanced through public credit facilities) in clearing more land, extending their acreage, using better tools, and so on, until they have quite important farms of 10, 20 or even more acres. To do this they have employed other people to work for them. Sometimes—but unfortunately not always—they have paid the Government minimum wages to these labourers for the period over which they were employed. The result has been an increase in production for the nation as a whole—that is, an increase in the amount of wealth produced in Tanzania—and a still further increase in the wealth of the man who owned, managed and initiated the larger farm.

The work of such people as this has shown that in the rural areas of Tanzania it is possible to produce enough crops to give an agricultural worker a decent life, with money for a good house and furniture, proper food, some reserve for old age, and so on. But the moment such a man extends his farm to the point where it is necessary for him to employ labourers in order to plant or harvest the full acreage, then the traditional system of ujamaa has been killed. For he is not sharing with other people according to the work they do, but simply paying them in accordance with a laid-down minimum wage. The final output of the farm on which both employer and employees have worked is not being shared. The money obtained from all the crops goes to the owner; from that money he pays 'his' workers. And the result is that the spirit of equality between all people working on the farm has gone—for

the employees are the servants of the man who employs them.
Thus we have the beginnings of a class system in the rural
areas. Also, the employees may well be paid for working
during harvest or during weeding but get no money for the
rest of the year.

Let us take an example. A cotton farmer in the Lake
Region who works hard and follows all the rules of good
husbandry will probably be able to cultivate 3 acres of
cotton, in addition to food crops, with just the labour of
his own family—assuming that all members will help to
pick when the cotton is ready. If he really produces 1,500
lb. to an acre—which some people have already exceeded—
and the price he receives after deductions is 46 cents a
pound, he will receive Shs. 2,070/- cash. From this he has
only to pay his District Taxes; his food is growing, his
house is his own and he has no rent to pay, and so on.
Apart from a minimum of clothes, repairs to his house,
and perhaps very low school fees, the money is at his
disposal to spend as he likes. Let us now assume that this
man decides that the following year he will plant 6 acres.
For this he and his family will have to work harder, but in
addition they will employ 3 people during the picking and
cleaning for an average period of 3 months during the year.
He will thus have to pay out to his labourers something like
Shs. 900/-; but in return—because he has used them—he
and his family will receive another Shs. 2,070/-. The
following year he will thus have Shs. 3,240/- to spend as he
likes. He can either expand further—perhaps by acquiring
a tractor, or other improved implements—or he can live
better, and so on. But the three men whose work at a
crucial stage made this extra Shs. 1,170/- possible, will have
received between them Shs. 900/- and for the rest of the year
they will have to depend upon other kinds of wage employment or find some other way of getting minimum food,

clothes and shelter. The one man is progressing very fast—and with increasing speed—and the others are receiving less than they could receive if they worked on their own account.

## The Implications of this Kind of Development

If this kind of capitalist development takes place widely over the country, we may get a good statistical increase in the national wealth of Tanzania, but the masses of the people will not necessarily be better off. On the contrary, as land becomes more scarce we shall find ourselves with a farmers' class and a labourers' class, with the latter being unable either to work for themselves or to receive a full return for the contribution they are making to the total output. They will become a 'rural proletariat' depending on the decisions of other men for their existence, and subject in consequence to all the subservience, social and economic inequality, and insecurity, which such a position involves.

Certainly at the moment everyone has a choice between working for others or farming on his own. In Tanzania's circumstances it may therefore seem unnecessary to be worrying about the implications of agricultural capitalist development—implications which will not reveal themselves in their full force until a shortage of land becomes a problem for our nation. But there are already local shortages of land in popular, fertile and well-watered areas. And in any case, if we allow this pattern of agriculture to grow, we shall continue to move further and further away from our goal of human equality. The small-scale capitalist agriculture we now have is not really a danger; but our feet are on the wrong path, and if we continue to encourage or even help the development of agricultural capitalism, we shall never become a socialist state. On the contrary, we shall be continuing the break-up of the traditional concepts of human equality based on sharing all the necessities of life and on a universal obligation to work.

There is, however, another institution in rural life which has brought a very great change to many of our peasants, and which does stem from the socialist principles of avoiding the exploitation of man by man. A large part of our farm produce is now marketed by co-operative societies which are owned and governed by the farmers themselves, working together for their own benefit. Many criticisms have been made of the workings of our co-operative societies; much practical improvement is necessary if they are really to serve the farmers and not to replace the exploitation of man by man by the exploitation of inefficiency and bureaucratic dishonesty. Yet there is no doubt that marketing by farmers, without the intervention of middlemen who are endeavouring to pay as little as possible to the farmer and receive as much as possible from the consumer, can be to the benefit of both the farmers and the rest of the community. In criticizing the working of existing co-operative societies, we must not make the mistake of blaming the principles of co-operation. The problems of co-operatives are practical ones, which must be worked out and dealt with by better and more skilled management and commercial machinery.

But although marketing co-operatives are socialist in the sense that they represent the joint activities of producers, they could be socialist institutions serving capitalism if the basic organization of agricultural production is capitalist. It is not inconsistent with the capitalist philosophy of the United States of America that farmers' co-operatives exist there and are quite strong. For a farmers' co-operative marketing society is an institution serving the farmers; if they are capitalist farmers, then the existence of a co-operative marketing society will mean that one group of capitalists—the farmers—are safeguarding their own interests, as against another group of capitalists—the middlemen. It is only if the agricultural production itself is organized on a socialist pattern that co-operative marketing societies are serving socialism.

## Summarizing the Present Position

At this point let us try to sum up the present position in Tanzania in a few words. We have the vast majority of our people living in the rural areas, most of them working on their own as farmers who do not employ any labour, but produce their own food and some additional crops which they sell. Many of them try to adopt modern methods, each on his own particular farm and while working in isolation. This is like every worker trying to have his own factory! There are, in addition, a small number of agricultural employers; a few of these are estates employing some hundreds of workers, but increasingly (although still in small numbers) the employers are individuals employing a few people for perhaps only part of the year. Here and there over the country we do have groups of people working on terms of equality and sharing the proceeds in co-operative farms, but these groups are so small in number that they do not yet make a real impact either on our total agricultural output or, except locally, on the social structure which is developing. They are important only as examples of what could be, not as an indication of what is.

Thus we still have in this country a predominantly peasant society in which farmers work for themselves and their families, and are helped and protected from exploitation by co-operative marketing arrangements. Yet the present trend is away from the extended family production and social unity, and towards the development of a class system in the rural areas. It is this kind of development which would be inconsistent with the growth of a socialist Tanzania in which all citizens could be assured of human dignity and equality, and in which all were able to have a decent and constantly improving life for themselves and their children.

## *Tanzania as it must develop*

For the foreseeable future the vast majority of our people will continue to spend their lives in the rural areas and continue to work on the land. The land is the only basis for Tanzania's development; we have no other. Therefore, if our rural life is not based on the principles of socialism our country will not be socialist, regardless of how we organize our industrial sector, and regardless of our commercial and political arrangements. Tanzanian socialism must be firmly based on the land and its workers. This means that we have to build up the countryside in such a way that our people have a better standard of living, while living together in terms of equality and fraternity. It also means that, in the course of time, the advantages of town life in the way of services and personal pleasures and opportunities must become available to those who work in the rural sector as much as those in urban areas.

If we are to succeed in this, certain things are essential. The first of these is hard work by our people. There is no substitute for this, especially as we do not have large accumulations of capital which can be invested in agricultural labour-saving devices or in increased productivity. We have to increase the amount we produce from our land, and we shall have to do it by the use of our own hands and our own brains. No organization of society can do away with this; whether we are capitalist, socialist, communist, fascist, or anything else, only an increase in output can provide the extra goods needed for our people to have the opportunity for a good life. The type of social organization we adopt affects both the distribution of the goods we produce and the quality of the life our people can lead, but it is irrelevant to the central fact that our output of goods has to be increased. Each person has to produce more by harder, longer, and better work.

It is not enough, however, for agricultural production to be increased. Marketing must be properly organized so that, even while our nation is in the grip of international market forces which control world prices, still we get the maximum possible for our goods, and our producers— that is, our farmers—get a fair return for their contribution to the national wealth. The co-operative movement in particular must be made more efficient, both in management and in its democratic machinery.

Not only this, there must also be an efficient and democratic system of local government, so that our people make their own decisions on the things which affect them directly, and so that they are able to recognize their own control over community decisions and their own responsibility for carrying them out. Yet this local control has to be organized in such a manner that the nation is united and working together for common needs and for the maximum development of our whole society.

And finally, the whole rural society must be built on the basis of the equality of all Tanzanian citizens and their common obligations and common rights. There must be no masters and servants, but just people working together for the good of all and thus their own good.

We shall be unable to fulfil these objectives if we continue to produce as individuals for individual profit. Certainly a man who is working for himself and for his own profit will not suffer from exploitation in this employment

But neither will he make much progress. It is not long before an individual, working alone, reaches the limit of his powers. Only by working together can men overcome that limitation. The truth is that when human beings want to make great progress they have no alternative but to combine their efforts. And there are only two methods by which this can be done; people can be made to work together, or they can work together. We can be made to work together by, and for the benefit of, a slave owner, or by, and for the profit of, a capitalist; alternatively we can work together voluntarily for our own benefit. We shall achieve the goals we in this country have set ourselves if the basis of Tanzanian life consists of rural *economic and social communities where people live together and work together for the good of all*, and which are interlocked so that all of the different communities also work together in co-operation for the common good of the nation as a whole.

The principles upon which the traditional extended family was based must be reactivated. We can start with extended family villages, but they will not remain family communities, and they must certainly be larger communities than was traditionally the case. Also, modern knowledge must be applied by these communities and to them; and the barriers which previously existed between different groups must be broken down, so that they co-operate in the achievement of major tasks. But the basis of rural life in Tanzania must be the practice of co-operation in its widest sense—in living, in working, and in distribution, and all with an acceptance of the absolute equality of all men and women.

This is very different from our present organization of society, and requires a reversal of the present trend. We shall not achieve it quickly. It is different because it involves a determination to maintain human equality. It is different because its dominant characteristic would be co-operation, not competition, and its criteria for individual success would be good service, not the accumulation of private property. The question is how we can organize our activities now so as to eventually reach this goal.

## No Simple or Single Answer for all Circumstances

It is essential to realize that within the unity of Tanzania there is also such diversity that it would be foolish for someone in Dar es Salaam to try to draw up a blueprint for the crop production and social organization which has to be applied to every corner of our large country. Principles of action can be set out, but the application of these principles must take into account the different geographical and geological conditions in different areas, and also the local variations in the basically similar traditional structures. For example, in the Kilimanjaro Region not only is the practice of individual land-holding almost universal, but also there is no unused land on the mountain. This affects social attitudes and creates some family problems which do not exist in those parts of Tanzania where a young man can get land of his own quite near to his father's farm as soon as he is ready to start his own family. Again, some parts of our country suffer from great water shortage or uncertainty; their agricultural organization, their density of population—and thus their social organization—must inevitably take account of these facts, just as the organization in well-watered areas must take advantage of its greater potential. All these things affect what can be grown, and the degree of investment in land or implements which is necessary for a given output. It would be absurd to try and settle all these questions from Dar es Salaam, particularly as such variations as those of the type of soil sometimes occur within a very small area. Local initiative and self-reliance are essential.

The social customs of the people also vary to some extent. The Masai are traditionally a nomadic cattle people; their family structure, their religious beliefs, and other things, have been shaped by this fact. They are therefore somewhat different from the social beliefs and organization of, for example, the traditionally agricultural Wanyakyusa. The steps which will be necessary to combine increased output with social equality may therefore also vary; the important thing is that the methods adopted should not be incompatible with each other, and should each be appropriate for the attainment of the single goal in the particular circumstances.

Quite apart from these local considerations, however, there is another factor which would prevent one universally applied method being introduced. For there are some things of which the nation as a whole has great need, but which might not be in the particular interests of any one locality or any particular group of farmers. Thus, for example, it may be necessary for purposes of water control to have forests at the headlands of rivers, and to prevent cultivation or animal herding there. The farmers in these regions might easily feel that this is not in their interests—that they would be economically better off by farming such land rather than leaving it for trees from which no return can be expected for perhaps 50 years. Or, to take another example, tourism brings important foreign exchange into the country, but any individual farmer would prefer to kill off wild beasts which might eat his produce rather than protect them for other people to look at. Or, again, some crops demand heavy mechanization or other invest-ment if they are to be most economically produced. No single farmer could undertake such work on his own; even a co-operative group would have difficulties at the beginning because of the heavy initial capital requirements and the consequent big burden of debt they would be accepting.

For this kind of over-riding national need it is essential that there should be positive Government action in the field of agriculture, as in other aspects of the economy. There must be state forests and local authority forests of different kinds. There must be national parks controlled and run by the public, acting through Government or the local authority; there must be other areas in which shooting of game is prohibited or controlled. In addition there should be state farms or local authority farms which deal especially with those crops which can be grown most economically for export or for urban sale only on a mechanized or large-scale basis, or where a combination of research and development is required, as for example in the state cattle ranching farm at Kongwa.

In such cases as these traditional agricultural methods can have no place; they are not appropriate. The choice is really only between allowing a few wealthy individuals to undertake the profitable work, if they wish, or reserving all of it for state operation.

In Tanzania it is clear that as a general rule new developments of this kind should be operated by the public, although some private or joint private and public investment may be appropriate in certain cases where expertise or capital is an immediate problem. But certainly it is better that the workers in plantation agriculture should be employed by the community as a whole, or that the community should have a dominant voice in their wages and conditions. By such public or joint public and private employment, the workers on this kind of mass production farm can be sure of fair treatment, and can do their work knowing that any proceeds from the farm go to the community in general or are being used for further investment. The workers will be able to know that their efforts are not just benefiting company shareholders whom they do not know and who do nothing to make the enterprise a success.

Thus, included in the rural and agricultural organization of a socialist Tanzania, there must be some state or other public enterprises, operated under the control of appointed managers and employing labour just as the nationalized food mills do. But this should only be a small part of the agricultural sector in Tanzania. It should not be our purpose to convert our peasants into wage-earners, even on Government farms. To make our socialism and our democracy a reality we should instead adapt to modern needs the traditional structure of African society. We must, in other words, aim at creating a nation in which ujamaa farms and communities dominate the rural economy and set the social pattern for the country as a whole.

### Ujamaa Agriculture

In a socialist Tanzania then, our agricultural organization would be predominantly that of co-operative living and working for the good of all. This means that most of our farming would be done by groups of people who live as a community and work as a community. They would live together in a village; they would farm together; market together; and undertake the provision of local services and small local requirements as a community. Their community would be the traditional family group, or any other group of people living according to ujamaa principles, large enough to take account of modern methods and the twentieth century needs of man. The land this community farmed would be called 'our land' by all the members; the crops they produced on that land would be 'our crops'; it would be 'our shop' which provided individual members with the day-to-day necessities from outside; 'our work-shop' which made the bricks from which houses and other buildings were constructed, and so on.

Obviously such community activities would need to be organized, would need to have a 'manager' responsible for the allocation of tasks and their supervision. There would need to be a 'treasurer' responsible for the money earned and its administration, and a 'governing committee' which is able to take executive decisions in between general meetings. But all these people could come from among the community, and must do so if it is to be a real socialist unit. They would be members of the community, not outsiders, although at the beginning there may be an advantage in attaching to such schemes some technical and other advisers if the right kind of expert could be found.

Such groups are possible in Tanzania—indeed a few already exist. There is no need to wait for the Government to organize them and give all the instructions. Nor would it be sensible to expect everyone who joins such a group to be willing to think only of the community interest and never of his own. Such unselfishness is rare in man, and no social organization should be based on the expectation that all members will be angels. What is required is a sensible organization which can be shown to be to the benefit of all members. This can be done if every member has certain responsibilities to the community, and is able to see his benefits from it because they are benefits to himself and to his own village.

The essential thing is that the community would be farming as a group and living as a group; investment in the community farm would be investment in the farm of every member; investment in the village—such as a clean water supply—would be of benefit to every member. The return from the produce of the farm, and from all other activities

of the community, would be shared according to the work
done and to the needs of the members, with a small amount
being paid in taxes and another amount (which is determined by the members themselves) invested in their own
future. There would be no need to exclude private property
in houses or even in cattle; some energetic members may
wish to have their own gardens as well as share in the
community farm. The extent of the private activities may
well vary from one village to another, but always on the
basis that no member is allowed to exploit another—nor
to exploit a non-member—and that all must play a fair
part in the life of the community from which they all benefit.

Such living and working in communities could transform
our lives in Tanzania. We would not automatically
become wealthy, although we could all become a little
richer than we are now. But most important of all, any
increase in the amount of wealth we produce under this
system would be 'ours'; it would not belong just to one or
two individuals, but to all those whose work had produced
it. At the same time we should have strengthened our
traditional equality and our traditional security. For in a
village community a man who is genuinely sick during the
harvest would not be left to starve for the rest of the year,
nor would the man whose wife is ill find the children
uncared for—as he might do if he farms on his own.
Traditional African socialism always made such questions
as these irrelevant, and our modern socialism, by resting on
the same foundations, will also make them irrelevant. For
in each ujamaa village the man who is sick will be cared
for; a man who is widowed will have no difficulty in getting
his children looked after; the old, the unmarried, the
orphans and other people in this kind of trouble will be
looked after by the village as a whole, just as was done in
traditional society.

Group work of this kind, too, would almost certainly allow for greater production and greater services in the community, with a consequent benefit to all members. It would be possible to acquire some modern tools if the members were willing to invest in them; some degree of specialization would be possible, with one member being, for example, a carpenter who makes the tables, chairs, doors and other things needed by the community, and works on the land only during times of greatest pressure, like the harvest. Another member could be responsible for building work, another for running a nursery where children could be cared for and fed while most of the mothers are in the fields, and so on. By such division of labour arranged by the members according to their own needs, the villagers could make their whole lives more fruitful and pleasant.

*Ujamaa Socialism in Practice*

A nation of such village communities would be a socialist nation. For the essential element in them would be the equality of all members of the community, and the members' self-government in all matters which concerned only their own affairs. For a really socialist village would elect its own officials and they would remain equal members with the others, subject always to the wishes of the people. Only in relation to work discipline would there be any hierarchy, and then such officials would be merely acting for the village as a whole.

Let us take a example. It would be a meeting of the villagers which would elect the officers and the committee, and a meeting of the village which would decide whether or not to accept or to amend any detailed proposals for work organization which the committee had drawn up in the light of general directions given by earlier meetings. Let us assume that a forty-member village meeting agrees to

a cotton farm of 40 acres and a food farm of 40 acres.
It would be the committee's job to propose where in the
land available these different crops should be planted, and
to propose the times and organization of joint work on the
land. At the same time the committee would have to make
proposals for the other work which had been decided upon—
perhaps the digging of a trench for a future piped water
supply, or the making of a new road, or the improvement of
village drainage. These detailed proposals they would
bring to the next village meeting, and once they had been
accepted it would be a job of the officers to ensure that all
members carried out the decisions, and to report to a
general meeting any problems as they occurred. As the
village became more established and the need for a village
carpenter, or a village nursery, or a village shop became
more pressing, the committee would work out proposals
as to how these could be organized and run by a member
for the common benefit. The village officials would also be
responsible for liaising with other villages and with the
general machinery of Government. Thus they would be
responsible for making any requests for outside assistance
about schooling, credit, agricultural advice, and so on,
which the village had decided it needed, as well as arranging
the selling of crops, the organization of taxes, payments, etc.

By such means as these there would be re-established
all the advantages of traditional African democracy,
social security and human dignity, and at the same time we
would have prepared ourselves to take advantage of modern
knowledge and the advantages which this can bring. For
there is no reason why, in the course of time, such villages
should not become more than simple agricultural communities, selling their crops and buying everything manu-
factured from outside. Certain things will always be
available more cheaply if they are mass produced; but

an established village could easily organize the production of other things for itself. And in co-operation with other nearby villages of the same kind, a system of locally based small industries would be possible for the benefit of all involved. Thus a group of villages together could organize their own servicing station for agricultural implements and farm vehicles; they could perhaps make their own cooking utensils and crockery out of local materials, or they could organize the making of their own clothes on a communal basis. Such villages could also organize together for social, political and educational purposes, so as to bring to all members in their rural area some of the opportunities which can come from living in communities. But all these things would depend upon the democratic decisions of the members themselves. The Government or local authority would become involved only where a decision involved them in responsibilities—as, for example, in the provision of a teacher if a school were planned, or where a proposal might affect the interests of people outside the village or villages directly concerned.

Government personnel and the local government would, of course, have a definite role to play in a society organized on the basis of such communal villages. Just as each village would be able to do certain things on its own, and for others would benefit from co-operating with similar villages nearby, so there are some things in which the nation as a whole has to co-operate. National defence, education, marketing, health, communications, large industries—for all these things and many more, all of Tanzania has to work together. The job of Government would therefore be to help these self-reliant communities and to organize their co-operation with others.

But it would certainly be easier for the members of the villages to take full advantage of Government's services

and to co-operate with their fellow citizens if they are
living and working together in their small groups. An
agricultural field worker, for example, would be teaching
new techniques to about 40 people together, instead of
one family at a time; he could thus spend more time and
give more expert help to the village farm than he could
ever give to any individual farmer. Or, again, Government
could not hope to give a water pump to every separate
house in a scattered community, nor provide the miles
of pipes which might be necessary in order to service one
isolated house. But it would be able to co-operate much
more quickly in the supply of a pump or pipes for a village
of 30 or 40 familes who were willing to do the physical
labour themselves.

The country would also become more democratic through this organization of ujamaa communities.
The Member of Parliament, or of the Local Council,
would more easily be able to keep informed of the people's
wishes and their ideas on national issues if they are living
together than if the people do not get a daily opportunity
to discuss important issues together. This means that
not only would the people be governing their own lives
directly in village matters, but they would also be playing a more effective role in the Government of their
country.

*How do we get to this Position?—Persuasion not Force*

It is one thing to argue the advantages of this type of
rural organization; the question is how can we move from
our present position to make it into a reality? The farmers
in Tanzania, like those elsewhere in the world, have learnt
to be cautious about new ideas however attractive they may
sound; only experience will convince them, and experience
can only be gained by beginning.

Yet socialist communities cannot be established by compulsion. It may be possible—and sometimes necessary —to insist on all farmers in a given area growing a certain acreage of a particular crop until they realize that this brings them a more secure living, and then do not have to be forced to cultivate it. But living together and working together for the good of all is not just a question of crop output. It depends on a willingness to co-operate, and an understanding of the different kind of life which can be obtained by the participants if they work hard together. Viable socialist communities can only be established with willing members; the task of leadership and of Government is not to try and force this kind of development, but to explain, encourage, and participate. For a farmer may well be suspicious of the Government official or party leader who comes to him and says: 'Do this'; he will be more likely to listen to the one who says: 'This is a good thing to do for the following reasons, and I am myself participating with my friends in doing it'. Individuals can have a very great effect in this work, whether or not they have any official position. Government can help to get such communities established by encouragement, and by giving priority in service to those groups who have committed themselves to this type of development. But it is vital that whatever encouragement Government and TANU give to this type of scheme, they must not try to run it; they must help the people to run it themselves.

It would also be unwise to expect that established farmers will be convinced by words—however persuasive. The farmers will have to see for themselves the advantage of working together and living together before they trust their entire future to this organization of life. In particular, before giving up their individual plots of land they will wish to see that the system of working together really benefits everyone. Groups of young men may be willing to experiment and this should be welcomed; we must encourage such young people. But what we are really aiming at is balanced communities where young and old are all involved together. Progress may thus be quite slow at the beginning, yet that is no reason for surrendering the goal. The man who creeps forward inch by inch may well arrive at his destination, when the man who jumps without being able to see the other side may well fall and cripple himself.

## Step-by-Step Transformation

Where necessary, then, progress can be made in three stages. The first may be to persuade people to move their houses into a single village, if possible near water, and to plant their next year's food crops within easy reach of the area where the houses will be. For some people in Tanzania this will be quite a change in living habits, so that in certain areas this may be the second rather than the first stage in the progress. For another step is to persuade a group of people—perhaps the members of a ten-house cell—to start a small communal plot (or some other communal activity) on which they work co-operatively, sharing the proceeds at harvest time according to the work they each have done. Alternatively, it might be that the parents of children at a primary school start a community farm, working together with the children, and jointly deciding what to grow and how to share out the proceeds. In either of these cases, and whether or not the people are living together in a village at this stage, the people would keep their individual plots; the community farm would be an extra effort instead of each family trying to expand its own acreage. Once these two steps had been effected, the final stage would come when the people have confidence in a community farm, so that they are willing to invest all their effort in it, simply keeping gardens around their own houses for special vegetables, etc. Then the socialist village will be really established and other productive community activities can get under way.

It is obvious, however, that with the variations in potential, in soils and in social customs, it would be absurd to set down one pattern of progress or one plan which must be followed by everyone. What is necessary is the objective of an ujamaa community. The interim steps and the detailed organization should be adapted to the local circumstances—which includes an understanding of the people's traditional attitudes as well as the degree of the people's political understanding and their acceptance of this social objective.

The important thing is that the work should begin. For this it is no use waiting for the Ministry of Lands, Settlement and Water Development to send out its officers to lay out villages, to explain, and so on. If this type of organization is to spread, every rural worker who understands the objective must play his part. The TANU cell leader may in some cases be able to persuade the members in his cell to make a beginning; the Agricultural Officer may be able to persuade a group of farmers how much more he would be able to help them if they were living and working together; the Community Development Officer who has won the confidence of the people in his area may be able to do it; or the TANU official at any level. The teacher in a primary school could help, or any individual Tanzanian who understands (even if he is a Sheikh or a Padre), and whether or not he has an official position. The important thing is that everyone should understand that this is no alternative to hard work; it is simply a more intelligent and more productive form of hard work which, if the weather is good, will lead to better results for all those participating. Promises of miracles, even promises of great Government help, will only lead to disaster.

The first few years of ujamaa village living will be very hard. The facilities available to the people will not immediately increase by their coming together, and there will be new problems of organization and co-operation. The wealth of each village will not be greater than that of the people at present, and the new possibilities—the vision of what can come in the future—may tempt the members to be more dissatisfied than they are at the moment, and to give way to the temptations of impatience. These socialist villages must grow from an application of the principle of self-reliance; they must grow through the efforts of their own members, and that means hard work which brings results only after a few years. Only a full realization of the problems as well as the possibilities of ujamaa communities will enable them to get firmly on their feet. This is why it is so important that each community should start with a mixture of private and co-operative living if the former has been the custom of the people, gradually increasing the level of co-operative working as the members sort out the problems which occur and find a method of organizing their communal activities which best suits them.

This is not to say that the different Ministries of Government have no role to play. But the basis of the growth of such ujamaa communities, and of their strength, can only be the work and the understanding of the participants. Government advice and help can only be of marginal importance; it must not be expected everywhere, for if all our two million families started such communities, it would clearly be impossible to help all their schemes at once. Even without everyone starting such schemes, the Government will not be able to give much help to any one that is established.

## *Distribution of Returns in an Ujamaa Village*

It is also important that the principles on which any returns from the community farm will be distributed should be just, simple and easily understood from the beginning. The basis must be to share according to the work done, for although in a family everyone shares equally whether they turned out for work every day or not, energetic people would understandably be unwilling to carry lazy people who were not members of their own family. Yet at the same time some proportion of the total return, at least once the village is properly established, should be set aside to help those in genuine difficulties—the sick, the crippled, the old, and orphaned children. It is also important that from the beginning the idea of putting some part aside for expansion or investment should be accepted. When the farm first begins, it might be possible in certain places for most of the return to be devoted to communal purposes, like buying pipes for water supplies, or building a new classroom, a community centre, and so on. This will be especially true while people keep their individual plots, although even here some personal return commensurate to the work done will probably be necessary.

All such decisions, however—how to share out as well as how much to grow, the arrangements for the children, the crippled and old—must be made by the agreement of all the participants. Village democracy must operate from the beginning; there is no alternative if this system is to succeed. A leader will have an opportunity to explain his ideas and to try to persuade the people that they are good; but it must be for the people themselves to accept or reject his suggestions. It does not matter if the discussion takes a long time; we are building a nation, and this is not a short-term thing. For the point about decisions by an ujamaa village is not just whether the members do or do not decide to dig a well or clear a new shamba. The point is that by making this decision, and then acting upon it, they will be building up a whole way of life—a socialist way of life. Nothing is more important than that, and it is not the work of a few days, nor of a few people. An ujamaa village is the village of the members, and the life there is their life. Therefore everything which relates exclusively to their village, and their life in it, must be decided by them and not by anyone else.

## Some Special Problems: Local Land Shortages

There are, however, some areas where local land shortage makes it impossible to move towards co-operative living and working through the opening of entirely new community farms. In such areas as Kilimanjaro for example, every piece of land is already intensively cultivated, with barely enough open spaces left for public purposes like schools, community centres—and so on. Furthermore, these areas are almost always farmed on the basis of individual plots, usually with each farmer living on his own plot and not in villages with his neighbours.

In areas like these there is already a social problem. Young men and women find that there is no work for them to do on their father's land, and no place nearby where they can start to farm on their own. Up to now they have, as a result, tended to drift to the towns looking for wage employment—which they are often unable to find. There is no easy answer to this; the only answer is through new settlements in other areas. It is impossible to expand the land on the mountain, and the only way forward for the growing population is to go to some other parts of Tanzania and start afresh. This is necessary whatever form of agricultural organization is adopted. Government must help the extra population from these areas to settle and to farm.

In the future, however, this assistance for re-settlement should be on the basis of settlement in villages which can develop into ujamaa communities. This does not mean that the Government should build modern expensive houses and complete villages for the new settlers to move into. That assumption has been our mistake in the past. Instead we must organize two 'moving days'. The first should be during the beginning of the dry season when active men and women are taken to the new area and loaned tents for a few weeks while they build temporary houses for themselves and their families, who will move in later and begin land clearing ready for the rains. When accommodation is ready the second 'moving day' should be instituted, with the families brought to begin their new life in the village.

For those people whose relatives cannot help them, the Government should provide food until the first harvest; it should also provide simple tools on credit, and be prepared to provide credit for poles, permanent roofing, etc., for the houses, and give a grace period of three years before repayment begins. In such settlements, too, it would be essential that agricultural advice be available, because the farmers would be unfamiliar with the crops and the soil requirements of the new area.

It is in circumstances like these that Government should try to provide a Community Development Officer or a TANU official familiar with the potential of living and working together, who would help the new settlers in the initial organization of their village committees, etc. Even so, if the new settlers come from areas of exclusively private farms, it would be a mistake to exclude individual plots at the beginning. Some large areas of land should be reserved for a community farm, but if the settlers wish it they should be allowed to clear first—although as a group—the land which they will each cultivate privately. In order to avoid the need for big capital investment, it is also necessary that the first effort should be made in the direction of the village growing its own food; land clearing and planting of cash crops should be the second priority, not the first.

The need for new settlement from areas of land shortage does not mean that the land shortage areas should be excluded from socialist development. It must be accepted, however, that socialist progress in these areas will be more difficult to achieve, for when vacant land is not available there is only one way to create a community farm; that is by individual farmers coming together and joining their pieces of land and working them in common. Furthermore, many of these areas are under permanent crops, like coffee. A farmer entering an ujamaa village under these circumstances will thus be investing at least part of his existing capital in the new project, not simply investing his effort in making an expanded farm. This will mean that a greater amount of socialist and technical education will be necessary before the first steps are undertaken, for the farmer must be convinced that working together with others, pooling his coffee trees with others, will still bring greater benefits to himself and his family.

It may be that the way to start under these circumstances is to operate first on the basis of working groups, but with the individual plots retained—that is, on the basis of mutual help. This would be simply a revival, and perhaps an extension, of the traditional system of joint activity, making it applicable to existing farms and not just to land clearing or house building. By working together on their private farms the farmers will be able to finish different jobs more quickly, or to do things which would be too difficult for any of them individually. They will then have time to do other useful things—either by themselves or co-operatively.

This first step of mutual help can be followed by others. The farmers could buy certain essential goods co-operatively —things like fertilizers, for example—or they could together build a store for their coffee, or something else which is of use to them all. By doing such things together the farmers will be gradually moving towards an acceptance of ujamaa socialism.

In areas of land shortage like this, the way for people to begin to work together may, however, not be in agriculture at all. Instead, a group of them may come together to start a small 'industrial' or 'service' project in which they all work for the good of all. Thus, for example, in Kilimanjaro a group of farmers may get together and jointly organize and run a modern poultry unit, or a communal tannery, or a communal woodwork shop. Or, again, they may come together to share the use of a truck which they jointly own, or to organize some new irrigation— perhaps with a water-wheel which they jointly own—which will benefit all of them. If people start working together in this way, it will be possible for these densely populated areas to become areas of rural industrialization, thus reducing their dependence on world prices of their cash crops, and also providing a new impetus to community activity and community life.

Rural industrialization projects must not be thought of in terms of large modern factories, but more in terms of 'cottage industries'. Yet it would be a mistake for such work to be done by separate families in their own homes; if the shirt-making or the knitting of sweaters and blankets is to be the project for a particular group, they should work together in one place so that they can help each other and each specialize on certain aspects of the work. Neither should great capital investment be considered. We have many traditional manufacturing activities which we can revive, and which we should revive. Government also intends to take further steps which we hope will, in a year or so, enable advice and ideas to be given to people in circumstances like these. But the important thing is that such 'village industries' must be organized and run on the same basis as community farms, that is, with the members making their own decisions, electing their own officers, and sharing the proceeds in accordance with what they themselves believe to be justice.

## Animal Husbandry Areas

Another special problem may well occur in those areas where animal herding is an important economic activity, if not the only one. Certainly no one can expect that all the farmers in such an area will straight away merge their herds into a common pool. But here, too, we can start gradually and build up socialist herding step by step while the farmers learn the full benefits of it. First we can start by mutual help in herding; the herders will mix up a group of farmers' cattle and take them all out together so that a smaller number of people are out at any one time. This, in fact, is quite customary for many of our people, and it would be comparatively simple to introduce the system where it has died out or never been practised. And it will mean that each farmer will have a little more time to do other work, either on his own or—better still—in co-operation with others for the benefit of the community as a whole.

Another method of advance is for a number of cattle-owners to each contribute one or two head of cattle so as to make up a community herd, which is then cared for by modern methods and which perhaps has a reserved grazing area. Each farmer would, at this stage, also keep his own herd. But gradually the improvement of the community herd, and the visible experience of communal benefits from it will probably lead them to build up the community herd and reduce the size of their separate cattle ownership. The participants would, of course, use the income from the community herd as they please. They may decide to use the milk for school feeding; they may decide that the income from the herd should be used to build a cattle dip, or a dam which will provide regular water for people and cattle alike; or they may decide to spend the income on improving the village or helping those members of their community who are in some kind of trouble.

In both of these special circumstances the move into a village, so that people live together as well as work together, may have to be accomplished gradually. But until it is done, real democratic and socialist living is impossible.

### Problem of Capital

A very important fact about this method of gradual progress into ujamaa communities is that there is no necessity for great capital investment before they can start. They can be, and—except where a completely new area is being started up to deal with people moving from over-populated areas—should be, started by the people from their own efforts. New land can be cleared by people using their own tools—the tools they use now on their individual plots. Often they themselves will be able to provide the seed for the community farm from their own stocks, or they can get an advance for the purchase of seed, fertilizers, etc., from their co-operative society or perhaps from the National Development Credit Agency. On that basis alone they can start, and the first year's profits from the community farm can then be used to purchase simple tools—perhaps an ox-plough—and so on, for expanded community effort in the coming years. Again, if there is a Savings and Credit Society existing in the area— and these should be encouraged whether or not there is an ujamaa community—the members of that society may agree to lend their savings for the purpose of starting or expanding an ujamaa community. The important thing is that there should be no reliance on great outside capital injection. We have already seen (in the original Government Settlement Schemes) the great dangers of heavy initial capitalization and the great burden of debt which it leaves for the farmers. And the truth is that in any case our nation does not have large amounts of capital. We have to create our own, and we can do this if we work together using at the beginning simply the resources we already have—that is, our labour, our land, and our willingness to work together.

## The Role of Government

Ujamaa villages will have to be established, and will grow through the self-reliant activities of our people. They will be created by the village people themselves, and maintained by them. It must be done from their own resources.

The Government's role is to help people to make a success of their work and their decisions. Further, where a village community has been established, the Ministry of Agriculture and Co-operatives should ensure that the necessary agricultural advice—about the best crops to plant on the community farm, and how to plant them for greatest success—is available to the villagers. If necessary, in a large village an Agricultural Field Officer could be stationed permanently so that his advice is available whenever required. Alternatively, if there is a member of the scheme who is qualified to receive special training, the Ministry must provide training for him; it must make available a place at an existing institution, or run special courses for such people.

The Ministry of Local Government and Rural Development, too, must be active in these villages; their field workers should be available to help the people to organize themselves, to advise them on how they can become eligible for advances for seed, or for small loans for farm equipment. It would be this Ministry, too, which should draw up a model constitution for the villages at different stages, although it must be stressed that no one model should be imposed on any village. Any model which is drawn up should just be a guide which draws the attention of the people to the decisions which have to be made by them; each village community must be able to make its own decisions. Nonetheless, the experience of existing ujamaa villages, such as those now operating within the Ruvuma Development Association, could be helpful, and the Ministry of Local Government and Rural Development should try to make this experience available to people from different parts.

But the most important thing is not that the Government should do this or that for all villages, but that within its resources it should give priority to requests which are received from villages where the people are living together and working together for the good of all.

## Conclusion

What is here being proposed is that we in Tanzania should move from being a nation of individual peasant producers who are gradually adopting the incentives and the ethics of the capitalist system. Instead we should gradually become a nation of ujamaa villages where the people co-operate directly in small groups and where these small groups co-operate together for joint enterprises.

This can be done. We already have groups of people who are trying to operate this system in many parts of our country. We must encourage them and encourage others to adopt this way of life too. It is not a question of forcing our people to change their habits. It is a question of providing leadership. It is a question of education. And it is a question of all of us together making a reality of the principles of equality and freedom which are enshrined in our policy of Tanzanian socialism.

# 8

# After the Arusha Declaration

*Presidential Address to the TANU National Conference,*
*17 October 1967*

Many things have happened since our last meeting, and
it is the job of this Conference to examine the most important of them in the light of the objectives we set ourselves
when we adopted the Arusha Declaration. For that Declaration was a commitment to the principles of self-reliance
and socialism. It did not by itself bring either of these things;
only hard thinking, and hard work in the right direction
will do that. It is important that we should be very clear
about this fact. The Arusha Declaration did not cause
miracles. It did not make the crops more fruitful, nor
the rains more regular. It did not make everyone wealthy,
nor change the level of our education. It did not change
the habits of mind we have grown up with, nor create any
other miraculous changes in our condition.

Our acceptance of the Arusha Declaration was like a
young Christian's confirmation; it is a declaration of intent
to live a certain kind of life and to act in a certain kind of
manner for desired ends. We have no more become a
socialist country because of the Arusha Declaration than
a young boy becomes a good Christian or a good Muslim
by the act of dedication. The sincere act of dedication is
important; but much more important are the actions which
follow during his life. The question before us, therefore,
is whether we have started to make the right decisions,
and the right plans, and whether we have begun to act in a

manner which will in time build socialism and self-reliance
in Tanzania.

First, let us look at this question of self-reliance, for I
believe that this has been widely misunderstood—by
ourselves more than by others. Some of our people have
spoken and acted as though it meant self-sufficiency in
manpower and financial resources. It means nothing
of the kind. We would be extremely silly if we imagined
that the Arusha Declaration had caused us to have more
qualified doctors, engineers, teachers, administrators,
and so on, so that the Development Plan target of self-
sufficiency in skilled manpower by 1980 had suddenly
become irrelevant. Self-reliance does not mean that,
for self-reliance is not a silly thing. Let us therefore be very
clear what we do expect now, and what the policy of
self-reliance means in the immediate future, and what it
does not mean.

First, it means that we must make maximum use of the
resources which we have. We want citizens to be given
priority in every field as soon as they are capable of doing
the job efficiently. And certainly we must have Tanzanians
making policy; Tanzanians must control our country.
But this is not an issue now; we have already achieved that.
The question at issue is whether we must at all costs have
Tanzanian citizens in every executive position. And the
answer we give must be a realistic one if we wish to fulfil
our ambitions. For the truth is that we do not yet have
enough qualified and experienced Tanzanian citizens to
do all the jobs which have to be done if the policies we
Tanzanians have decided upon are to be implemented.

The question, therefore, is whether we are prepared to
make our plans wait until we have educated and trained a
Tanzanian for every job which has to be done. And we
long ago decided that this would not only be absurd, it

would also be unnecessary. An accountant is an accountant, whether he is a citizen or not; a doctor is a doctor; a manager is either efficient or not efficient. What really matters in relation to such people— whether they be citizens or not citizens—is that they loyally and efficiently carry out the decisions made by our Government and our people.

To employ an inefficient person just because he is a Tanzanian, when the job he has to do is crucial for our development, is not self-reliance; it is stupidity. When we or members of our family fall ill, what we want is a competent doctor, not necessarily a citizen. When we have decided to build a bridge, what we want is a competent engineer who will be able to ensure that the bridge will be safe and effective for its purpose.

The questions we need to ask ourselves are these. Firstly, is this job essential to our plans? Secondly, do we have a citizen who is qualified and has the necessary experience for this particular job? And if there is no qualified citizen available, thirdly, can we obtain a qualified non-citizen who will be accountable to us for his loyal and efficient carrying out of the job? And fourthly, what plans do we have for the training of citizens to do this kind of work in due course? Then, if we decide that the job is essential, and if there is no qualified citizen available to do it, and if a non-citizen can be obtained, let us pay a non-citizen to do the job for us. By doing this we might, for example, make it possible for a village in an outlying area to become self-reliant because it can sell its increased production and thus support improved conditions for its members. If we do not allow this bridge to be built simply because we have no citizen available to do it, then the village will remain on a low level and without any real possibility of becoming a self-reliant, prosperous community.

But in this country we also have a second thing which we really desire of the people working for us. Ideally we also need socialists in every job—which is not necessarily the same thing as wanting a citizen for every job, because not all Tanzanians are socialists. But if a competent doctor also has socialist attitudes, then he is surely an especially great asset to us. And the truth is that the international reputation of Tanzania is such that many socialists from other countries very much want to come and work with us. One day in the future Tanzanian socialists may be able to assist other socialists to achieve their objectives. Today we should be ready and happy to welcome socialists from other countries who are ready to help us achieve our objectives. And we should remember that many socialists come from capitalist countries; it is sometimes the very fact that they cannot contribute to socialist objectives in their own country which makes them enthusiastic about working with us.

What all this means is that if we are to make progress towards the implementation of our policies of socialism and self-reliance, we should be ready to use all the people who are able to contribute towards these objectives. There are certain jobs which have to be done by citizens. Those we have now filled. There are other jobs which have to be done, and done now or in the next few years, whether or not we have enough citizens or enough socialists. Let us get these jobs done instead of indulging our prejudices or our generalized assessments of people by skin colour or country of origin.

There is another aspect of our self-reliance policy which has also been misunderstood by some people. For the Arusha Declaration does not say that Tanzania refuses outside aid, or that there is something wrong in receiving it. The Declaration says, and I quote: 'We are not saying that we will not accept, or even that we shall not look for, money from other countries for our development. This is not what we are saying'. What the Arusha Declaration says is that the only group of people we will rely upon is ourselves; we will not organize our country and our life in such a way that there will be no development unless we get foreign money. And most of all, we have said very firmly that we shall not bend our political, economic or social policies in the hope of getting overseas aid as a result. But if we get outside assistance to carry out purposes decided by us, then we shall welcome that assistance. Thus we welcome the Chinese decision to help with the Tanzam Railway. Thus we shall welcome an American decision to help build our road from Dar es Salaam to Tunduma.

In fact, self-reliance is not really against anything or anyone, unless there are people who want to re-colonize us. Self-reliance is a positive affirmation that we shall depend upon ourselves for the development of Tanzania, and that we shall use the resources we have for that purpose, not just sit back and complain because there are other things we do not have.

We are saying to ourselves that we are going to build a self-reliant socialist society. We are saying: 'Here is land, here we are; this is the amount of knowledge, skill and experience we have; and this is the amount of money we have to spend on supplementing our skill and knowledge or on buying more advanced machines. Now let us get on with it.' And we are saying to other people: 'This is what we are doing; if you want to help us, do this and this and this, for that is what we need most at this stage'. The really important thing for us to be clear about is that we are not saying to other people (and now, after the Arusha Declaration, we cannot say): 'Please come and develop our country for us, and if you insist we will stop being

socialist, or believing in equality, or being anti-colonial'.
These things we will never say. We do not believe that
anyone else can develop our country for us and, even if
they could, we would not be willing to give up the determination of our own policy. It is we ourselves who will
develop our country. We may decide to spend some of the
resources we have, or the products of those resources, on
buying imports of skills or machines from abroad. But our
real emphasis will be on using the skills that we already
have, and in developing the natural resources that we now
possess.

In our situation this means that the emphasis of our development will be in the rural sector, and particularly in
agriculture. Further, it means that we shall modernize
within our resources. But we must modernize. In many
parts of the country we are beginning to follow the advice of
our agricultural experts. But our major tool, the jembe,
is too primitive for our present day needs. We must now
abandon it and replace it with the oxen-plough. We cannot
make progress by waiting until every peasant is able to
possess his own tractor which he can drive and maintain.
Indeed, if we wait for that we shall never leave the hoe
behind us, for our present methods are too inefficient ever
to produce the wealth which would enable us to buy
tractors for all parts of the country, or to train the people
to drive and maintain them. We are not ready for the
tractor, either financially or technically; but we are ready
for the oxen-plough. We have the animals, and the ploughs
can be bought cheaply or even made here. They are simple
tools which our peasants can quickly learn to use, and they
are appropriate for the kind of small unit farming which is
involved in the ujamaa villages to which we aspire, or even
to the amount of land an energetic individual peasant
family can cultivate.

We have to modernize our farming if we are to improve our standard of living. But we cannot modernize by buying tractors for everyone, because we do not have either the necessary money or the necessary technical skill, or the social organization which would make such implements economic. We have to modernize by utilizing to the full the tools which are within our capacity to buy and to make; which are sufficiently simple for us to use without trouble and breakdowns; and which are appropriate to our present and near future social and economic organization. And this we can do. The oxen-plough, the oxen-cart, the use of the donkeys which now eat our grass without working—all these things can make a tremendous improvement in our output and therefore in the lives of our people. We must move to these techniques with the maximum possible speed. Then, when we have effected this revolution all over the country, we shall be able to move from the oxen-plough to the tractor. But that time is not yet; now we have to concentrate our attention on the immediate objective.

This does not mean that we shall have no tractors or modern machinery working in Tanzanian agriculture. We shall have these things to deal with special problems, or working on large, highly organized state farms where there is all the work discipline of a modern factory. But they are not appropriate at the present time for the majority of our farming units; and in any case we cannot afford them, nor could we use them in such a way as to justify their expense.

For let us be quite clear. Self-reliance is not some vague political slogan. It has meaning for every citizen, for every group, and for the nation as a whole. A self-reliant individual is one who co-operates with others, who is willing to help others and be helped by them, but who does not depend on anyone else for his food, clothing or shelter.

He lives on what he earns, whether this be large or small, so that he is a truly free person beholden to no one. This is the position of the vast majority of our people now; it must be the position of all of us.

For a community, self-reliance means that they will use the resources and the skills they jointly possess for their own welfare and their own development. They will not take the attitude that the Government, or Local Council, or anyone else, must come and do this or that for them before they can make any progress. There will be things for which outside assistance in the form of skilled advice or a capital loan is necessary, but they will realize that this has to be paid for, directly or indirectly, by them and their fellow citizens. And outside capital assistance, in particular, will only be requested after all local development with local resources has been undertaken, and only to the minimum extent necessary to effect their purposes.

For the nation self-reliance will come if the individuals and the different communities are self-reliant, and if the citizens together recognize that their way forward must be determined by their joint resources and their common efforts. It means choosing the path to development which does not depend upon outsiders. It means a recognition of international involvement and a willingness to give and to receive help. It means a recognition that outside assistance can help to speed up development along the path which we have chosen. But it also means that the path itself must be one which is within our resources.

## The War against Exploitation

Of course, self-reliance was not the only point of the Arusha Declaration. The Declaration also declared war on exploitation of all kinds. The nationalization measures and the Government action to secure majority control in major economic enterprises was one part of the action which has been taken, and has to be taken, against exploitation in Tanzania. Another concern of the Government for many years has been the exploitation of wage-earners by their employers. The minimum wage legislation, the severance pay legislation, and many other Government and NUTA actions have removed the worst examples of this kind of exploitation, although the problem of enforcement still remains in many cases. But the problem which is now worrying many of our people is the prices of the goods we wish to buy in the shops, and the quality of those goods.

Government has established a National Advisory Board on Price Control as a major first step towards dealing with this problem. But we will be making a very big mistake if we just treat this problem in a negative fashion. The distribution of goods, whether they are made in Tanzania or imported, is a service which has to be paid for. It is no use our establishing textile factories in Dar es Salaam, Mwanza and Arusha if the people of Sumbawanga cannot get the cloth in their district and from their village shops. Someone has to arrange to transport that cloth and to hold it in the shop ready for the day when the peasant has some money and needs to buy new cloth for himself or his wife. This distribution service is just as important to the peasant as the actual production of the cloth. It cannot be handled by the state, and it is no use our laying down rules and regulations which are so restrictive that no one can earn his living by transporting the cloth to the outlying areas and selling it there. Yet at the same time we have to take account of the fact that the cost of selling this cloth is very different in Mwanza from what it is in Sumbawanga. There is no reason why a shopkeeper in this town should be allowed to charge the same price as the man in the south-west of our country—unless he is somehow being made to subsidize the extra cost of transporting locally made produce to far distant places.

What I am really saying here is that price control is not going to be easy. If we simply lay down hard and fast rules for everything, we may finish up with the farmer being unable to buy the things he wants at a convenient place —which is certainly no service to him, and is therefore not the way to prevent him being exploited. The best way to deal with this problem is for people to establish their own co-operative shops, controlled by them, where they can see the real cost of obtaining something at a convenient place. Then they will be able to ensure that they are paying the costs of distribution, but are not paying for certain people to live in idleness at their expense.

If we do this we may well find that prices in many areas do not come down very much. In 1962 the Government paid for an enquiry into the distribution business; we wanted to see how far it was possible to give better and cheaper service to our people. The conclusion of this enquiry was that, although there are some pockets of exploitation, especially where one shop has a local mono-poly, or where credit is given, Tanganyika had, on the whole, what they called a 'low cost distribution system'.

However, we were not satisfied that nothing could be done, and we tried to establish co-operative wholesale and retail shops by Government initiative. Then we dis-covered some of the problems for ourselves. Many of these co-operatives failed and the shops have had to be closed. The most important reasons for their failure were, in the first place, inexperienced and poor management, and in the second place, the high costs involved in paying reasonable wages to the shop workers. For the truth is that most of Tanzania's private shops, both African and non-African, are family businesses, where all members of the family share in the work and then, as a group, share in any profits. They have no fixed wage, and often earn less than they would if they had to receive the Government fixed minimum wage.

Yet this is no reason for giving up—because some exploitation does still continue. Price control for certain basic commodities is both necessary and practical, and it will be enforced—usually on a regional basis. But in addition, we should look again at the lessons of our experience in co-operative trading and see if we can make a fresh start. Previously these shops were started on Government initiative; they did not spring from the local community, so that the people felt neither loyalty to them nor confidence in them as weapons against exploitation. But suppose a village community, or the people in a group of streets, decided to start their own shop on an ujamaa basis; then it would really be their 'own' shop to which they had a loyalty. They could jointly decide what type of things they wanted to be available and they could arrange to share in the work, the expenses, and the profits of the shop they were using—just as we are suggesting they should do in relation to ujamaa farming.

If such shops start small, and deal first in the basic requirements of their area, without putting their prices too low while they are building up their capital, we may find that a co-operative retail system can grow and be of great service to us. This will only happen, however, if the shops spring out of the people; they cannot be organized for the people by the Government or anyone else. This is, in fact, another case where self-reliant development is the only practical way forward. And even if it does nothing else, the possibility of competition from an ujamaa co-operative will certainly discourage private shops from exploiting their customers. For it is not enough simply to say that the price of such and such a commodity is too high. We should be able to say that our co-operative shop sells this commodity at so much; therefore, if the shop next door charges more, its price is too high.

There is another way in which we can reduce the price we pay for the goods we buy in the shops. This is by moving away from the practice of buying almost everything on credit. Let there be a stated price of goods, and let that be a cash price, with the extra cost of credit clearly stated. Then our people will see how much it is costing them to borrow money from the shopkeeper in order to buy his goods—which is what we are doing when we buy goods on credit. In most cases there is really no need for credit buying. We buy on credit because we do not organize our income properly, or because we do not save enough money at the beginning of the month, or at the end of the harvest, to meet the kind of irregular payments which all of us get involved in at some time—things like school fees, wedding costs, burial costs, etc. This is a question of self-discipline. Organizing one's income properly is, of course, a particular problem of farmers, who receive money only once a year—when the crops are harvested and paid for. But such people, as well as wage-earners who are trying to buy some more expensive article, have a solution which they can develop for themselves. The Savings and Credit Co-operative Societies (Shirika za Akiba) can be of very great service, both to the individual and to his local community. Many of these societies already exist in Tanzania, but new ones should be started for they can help us very much in our individual and national drive towards self-reliance. Government has ten full-time workers in the Ministry of Agriculture and Co-operatives who are trying to encourage and help these societies; I hope that all TANU leaders will learn about them and see how and when the people in their area can be helped to establish them.

What all this means is that there are many different ways of working against exploitation in our country; and often the least effective are those which simply try to control or restrict the activities of other people. For I say again, it is not enough just to accuse our shopkeepers of exploitation. Instead, we have to organize ourselves for our own benefit, and then our shopkeepers will realize that it is to their own best interests to give honest service. The few who really try to abuse their position can then be—and will be—dealt with firmly by Government and people.

## Responsibilities of Leadership

In this field, as in so many others, what is called for is good, honest leadership from people who are really committed to the welfare of the citizens of Tanzania. And the kind of honest leadership which is required is not necessarily the noisiest. If a leader can encourage the people and help them to understand problems and policies by his constructive oratory, that is a very good thing. But it is not entertainment that our people want and expect from their leaders; nor do they want a lot of false promises about a Utopia which someone will bring to them; nor do they want to listen to their leader abusing some person or some group which he has set up as a scapegoat for the problems the people are experiencing.

The leaders of Tanzania—and that includes everyone present at this Conference, as well as many other people—have to show, in both actions and words, that they recognize one central fact. Leaders cannot do anything FOR the people. We can only provide the necessary information, guidance and organization for the people to build their own country for themselves. Leaders of Tanzania should not be making promises; we cannot fulfil them for others. We should not be complaining; complaints help no one. We should know the facts of Tanzania's situation, understand them, and give guidance to the people in the light of them.

This is essential. Leaders have to know the reality of our present position, and then show the people how, by our own efforts, we can change our present poverty into something better. It is no use pretending that certain facts are not facts; it is no use talking about 'alleged' low prices of sisal, etc., when the low world price of sisal is, and has been, a fact for many years and a fact which has very important implications for the plans we should be making. Bad things do not disappear because we pretend they are not there, or because we accuse other people of causing them. We cannot run this country by complaining, and we have been entrusted with the responsibility of running this country. Complaining that we are poor, or that world prices are low, is as useless as complaining that the rains do not fall. We have to assess our present situation—which includes many things beyond our control—and work out plans to change the situation and to counteract the effect of the things we cannot alter. Then we have to execute our plans by hard and intelligent work. There is no other way. There is no short cut.

Our people are poor. That is a fact. It is also a fact that every human being finds it easier to see the greater wealth or the greater privilege of other people than he does to see his own advantages. It is not part of a Tanzanian leader's duty simply to encourage the people in envy, or to turn that envy into hostility or hatred against others. But he does have to make it clear to the people that he is not himself among a group which is unfairly privileged. It is for this reason that the leadership qualifications have been laid down in the Arusha Declaration.

For at the very least it must be clear to our people that no leader will become wealthy by abusing his position or by exploiting others. They must know that any wealth he gains will be from wise use of the payment the people make to him in return for his service. But even this is not enough. Leaders must show the way to the development of our country and our people. If ten hunters have trapped a rabbit they are foolish idiots, wasting their energies, if they stop their hunting in order to fight over the distribution of the meat on that rabbit. They would do better to concentrate their energies on working out a better system of hunting so that they can increase the amount of meat available to them all.

That is similar to the position in Tanzania. This is a poor country now. We do not produce enough wealth for all of us to lead a decent life; we are like the ten hunters with one rabbit between them. There is no getting away from this fact. Neither is there any other way for us to increase our wealth except by producing more. In particular we must realize that it is no good our simply increasing the amount of money in the country. Government could easily order the Bank of Tanzania to print more notes and to give everyone a present of so many shilling notes every year. But this would not increase our wealth in the very slightest. The result would simply be chaos.

To get this truth quite clear in our minds, let us take a simplified example. Imagine a village of ten people in the Rufiji Delta which is cut off by floods. Between them these people have Shs. 1,000/- in notes. They also have one bag of rice. If the Government uses a helicopter to drop another Shs. 1,000/- in notes to these people, will they be any less hungry, less cold, or less in danger from the water? Or if the people decide to make a fire and to burn all the notes in the village, will they be any worse off? But suppose the Government drops more rice from the helicopter. In that case the people will have more to eat, quite regardless of the number of notes which they have between them. On the other hand, if there was an accident and the bag of rice was destroyed, then the people would be in serious trouble, regardless of the fact that they still had all their shilling notes. For they cannot eat notes, nor use them as shelter. Money is not wealth.

Of course, it would be a different situation if, in this isolated village, one person out of the ten managed to get hold of the extra Shs. 1,000/- which the Government dropped by helicopter. The total wealth of the ten men would not be any greater, but this particular individual would be able to get more of the rice for himself. The other nine would therefore get less rice because—let me say again—the amount of rice available would not have been increased by the importation of more money to this isolated community. If the lucky man getting all the extra money happened to be the poorest man in the village, then the effect might be that the distribution of the wealth (that is, the rice) was better as a result of the extra money coming in. In such a case the extra money would have been a substitute for a joint decision by the ten people to distribute the rice fairly. But if the man who got the extra money was already as well off as the majority, or even better off, then nothing at all good or socialist would have come out of the extra money being brought in.

### Our Wealth

It should not be necessary for TANU leaders to understand statistics before they realize that Tanzania is poor. We see, and we live with poverty. Yet sometimes our people get confused by the sight of a few individuals driving private cars, or by figures which the Minister for Finance talks about during the Budget, and they begin to believe that somehow and somewhere there is a lot of wealth in this country, and that the poverty they see around them is due to unequal distribution, or to exploitation, or even that the poverty does not really exist!

Let me therefore state, once again, what the real position is. If all the wealth of all the people in this country were put into one big heap, and then divided equally between all the people who live in Tanzania, each person would receive goods to the total value of Shs. 525/-. That is all he would have for a year. Not a month, but a year. This means that the total wealth of the country is valued at about Shs. 5,455,000,000/-. Out of that amount, nearly $10\frac{1}{2}$ million people have to eat and clothe themselves; we have to run our schools, our hospitals, maintain our roads and our houses, pay for our administration, pay our army and police forces, pay for our Government, and do every other single thing which we want to do in this country. But in addition, it is from this same amount that we have to invest for a better life in the future by building new roads and communications, by building factories, houses, new schools, and so on. In fact, the total wealth available to be spent by all the people of Tanzania during one year is much less than the amount which the Government of the United States of America spends on its military forces in one week. (This should be remembered by every well-off Tanzanian who likes to live in luxury).

However we divide our wealth between us, we are a poor nation. There is no getting away from that fact, and anyone who pretends otherwise by promising the people riches is trying to fool the people, and he should be condemned.

This does not mean that the distribution of our total wealth between different groups of people is unimportant. Of course it is very important, and one of the points made in the Arusha Declaration is that there must be greater equality of incomes between the different people of this country. All that I am concerned to stress here is that the amount which we have to distribute is small. We are like the ten hunters with one rabbit, whom I referred to earlier. Our major preoccupation must be to increase our wealth, and the amount of time and energy we spend on squabbling over what we now have should be very limited indeed.

But what have we in fact done, so far, as regards the distribution of incomes in Tanzania? And what are our plans for the distribution of the wealth we create—how do we propose to divide it fairly?

First, ever since independence we have been gradually making our taxation system more progressive, which means that the higher your income the greater proportion of it you pay in taxes. Thus, for example, there are only ten people in our whole country who have an income of Shs. 300,000/- or more in a year, and these people each pay more than two-thirds of that amount to the Government in direct taxation. After that the luxury goods they want to buy are also very heavily taxed. Of course they remain wealthy in comparison with the rest of us. But they are nothing like as wealthy as they would be if they lived in almost any other country of the world. And people with much lower incomes than that also feel the effect of our heavily progressive tax system—and quite rightly. Any senior civil servant, any Minister, or any other highly qualified worker in Tanzania will be willing to give you evidence of this, even if he is too much of a socialist to complain about it! Taxation policy is, and will be, a very important and very effective way of controlling income differentials in this country.

Second, we have put a stop to any future large-scale exploitation of our workers and peasants through the private ownership of the means of production and exchange. In February we rounded off a number of smaller measures which restricted opportunities for exploitation of this type by nationalizing the banks, the insurance business, a number of large firms involved in the food industry, etc. We cut these straws. At the same time we took control of a number of other businesses; in other words, we put our finger on the straw so as to control the amount which goes through it.

Thirdly, we have put a stop to wage and salary increases at the top levels and have even, in the case of people working directly for the Government, succeeded in cutting their incomes. Our job now is to make sure that the top wages of Tanzanians outside the Government sector also get involved in the high-level freeze. For however much our total national income is increased by our efforts in the coming years, it is highly unlikely that the increase will justify any addition to the top salaries in the foreseeable future.

But the number of people involved at this level is very small indeed; probably not more than 35,000 individuals get enough income to be liable to pay income tax, much less surtax. The real problem in Tanzania is not redistribution between the rich and the poor, but a fair distribution of wealth, and of contribution to national expenses, between the very poor and the poor, between the man who can barely feed himself and the man who can barely clothe himself. Yet even so, considerable improvements have been made for that group of our workers whose incomes can be fairly easily influenced by Government and by their own direct action—which is the wage-earners. The cost of employing a worker in Tanzania has more than doubled during the six years since 1961. Cash wages have increased considerably in most cases, and fringe benefits like leave, severance pay, employers' contribution to the Provident Fund, and so on, have all increased the real security and income of the wage-earner.

The incomes of the peasants, however, are not so susceptible to Government action. By encouraging the co-operative movement we have tried to avoid the exploitation of the peasants by middlemen; we are now engaged in trying to improve the efficiency and effectiveness of the co-operative movement so as to ensure that one type of exploitation does not get replaced by another—the exploitation of inefficiency and bureaucracy. Yet for the most part, the peasant's income in this country is determined by his own hard work, combined with the effect of the weather and the world prices of the crops he sells. Government can, and does, help the peasant by teaching new methods of planting, by making better seeds available, and within our resources by providing credit with which he can buy better tools or fertilizers, etc. But neither Government nor peasant can control the weather; nor can either of us control the prices which our exports receive in the world market.

It is true that some of the crops produced by our peasants are consumed within Tanzania, and that for many of these the Government fixes the price. This does not mean, however, that the Government can increase the wealth of our people by increasing the prices of the food crops. If, for example, we set a higher price for maize, what would be the effect? The result would be that the wage-earners who now buy the maize would have to pay more out of their existing incomes in order to eat the same amount. Their real incomes would thus have gone down. In other words, by increasing the incomes of the farmers, we would be decreasing the incomes of the wage-earners. The wage-earners would then naturally demand an increase in their wages on the grounds that the cost of living had gone up. If that demand were granted, the effect would be to increase the cost of the things the wage-earners produced—things like shirts, shoes, and so on, which the peasant buys. So in the end neither the peasant nor the wage-earner would be better off; both would have more money, but neither would have more goods than he had before.

There is no way of improving our incomes until and unless we improve our output. This can be seen very easily in the case of the peasant, because he works on his own land and owns the crops which he grows. He may complain about the prices he receives, just as he complains about the weather. But he can always see the connection between his output and his income. Whatever the price, if he succeeds in growing 12 bags of maize on an acre, he will be richer than if he only grows 4 bags of maize on that acre. Anything which the Government can do to contribute to the better yield on his land is a contribution to his income, provided that he does the necessary work himself.

For the wage-earners the same basic principles apply; output and income are connected. If the worker's income goes up while the value of his output does not go up, or if his income remains the same while the total value of his output goes down, he will then soon begin to get into difficulties. Let us take a simple case of 100 shirt-makers in a factory who produce between them, let us say, 2,000 shirts a month, that is, 20 for each worker. Let us further assume that each of these workers receives Shs. 200/- a month; on that basis the cost of producing each shirt will be Shs. 10/-. (In order to keep the example simple, I am leaving aside all questions of rent for the factory, cost of the machines, transport, etc., etc.). At that price all the shirts which are produced are bought by the consumers of Tanzania.

Let us now see what happens if the wage of each worker in this shirt factory is increased to Shs. 300/- a month without them increasing the number of shirts they produce. Each shirt would then cost Shs. 15/-. But the consumers only have sufficient money to spend Shs. 20,000/- on buying shirts; therefore, instead of 2,000 shirts being sold each month, only 1,333 shirts will be sold each month. But that means that 67 workers only are needed to produce the number of shirts which can be sold. The other 33 workers will be dismissed because no one can buy the goods they produce. The total effect of the increase in wages has therefore been that 67 people are better off; their incomes have increased from Shs. 200/- a month each to Shs. 300/- a month each. But 33 workers who used to receive Shs. 200/- a month each now receive nothing; in addition, the consumers of Tanzania only have 1,333 new shirts every month instead of having 2,000 new shirts every month.

This is, of course, a very simplified example; but it is not a false one. Indeed something like this has been happening in Tanzania since 1961. Altogether wage incomes have risen by something like 80 per cent, while the productivity of the wage-earners as a group has increased by very much less than this. As a result, 93,000 less people are now employed for wages than were employed for wages in 1961. Many of these people lost their jobs because it became less expensive for the employer to buy a machine than to spend money every month on the increased wages of the number of workers necessary to do the same job by hand. That means that in order to keep prices down, some employers sacked workers and bought a machine to do the same job. In many cases there was no alternative if they were to remain in business. In other cases—for example, in domestic employment—the employers did more work themselves; or they simply contracted their activity, because the higher wages made it uneconomic—the sisal industry gives many examples of this. In 1961 128,928 people were employed in the sisal industry, in 1966 the figure had fallen to 64,593, and now it is even lower.

The connection between wage increases without corresponding increases in productivity on the one hand, and the amount of employment available on the other, is very obvious from the statistics. Thus, for example, in 1963, when the overall wage levels increased most drastically, the number of people in employment dropped by more than any other year. In 1964, when wages rose slightly—probably by about the same amount as productivity increased—the number of people in employment actually increased. Let me put this in figures. Average wages rose by 28 per cent in 1963; and employment fell by 14 per cent. In 1964, on the other hand, average wages rose by about 3 per cent while the number of people in employment also increased by 3 per cent. Obviously the 1964 experience is more in keeping with our ambitions to expand the economy —and nearer to the target of the Development Plan which is for a 6 per cent per annum increase in employment.

Sometimes it is said that the increased wages should be paid out of profits, and that if this is done prices will not have to go up and nor will the peasants be any worse off—only the rich employers. Unfortunately, as I have already indicated, this is not true in Tanzania; it may be true in some other countries, but that is not our concern. The people of Tanzania, through their Government, their local government, their co-operatives, or through the publicly owned industries, are now the biggest employers of wage-earners in the United Republic. Any profits made

by publicly owned or controlled industries come back to
the people and are spent for our national development and
our national welfare. That was the point of the nationalization exercise in February. And it would certainly be
very unfair if the few people who happened to be lucky
enough to get jobs in a place like Williamson's Diamond
Mines (which is 50 per cent publicly owned) were to have
all the profits of that place paid out to them in wages.
Those profits must be shared amongst us all—and in fact
more than three-quarters of the profits of this industry
now come to the Government or to other national institutions.

Indeed the truth is that employees in Williamson's, and
places like it, are already a privileged group of wage-earners
receiving very much above the average rates for the kind
of work they are doing. We even had the ludicrous position
recently where the Government had to decide what to
do about a group of people who had been paid by Williamson's while they were on a special course, and who are now
pointing out that, by paying them only the wage we have
been paying to expatriate workers in another branch of the
diamond industry, they would be receiving less income for
doing the job than they had received while being trained for
it!

Wage-earners obtain their living by being part of a very
complex economic organization. They cannot be expected
to understand by instinct the very real connection between
their output, their wages and their continued employment.
It is our job—that is, the job of TANU and NUTA leaders
—to understand these things and to explain them. It is
our job to show the workers and peasants that there is
only one way in which we can increase the amount of wealth
available to us. That is by increasing the amount we produce.
Out of that increase we can then have a little more to spend
on ourselves and our immediate needs—whether these be

new schools and hospitals, or more wages for every individual. And the rest of the increased wealth we have created by our efforts we can devote to investments, so that it will be easier for us to increase production still more in future years. But we cannot increase wages or other incomes first and hope that increased production will follow. A farmer cannot eat his maize before he has cleared the ground, planted, weeded, and waited for the time when he can harvest his crop.

None of this means that we have done all there is to do in the way of equalizing the incomes in our country. But we must equalize incomes as we make our total wealth grow. It is growth which we must concentrate on. We must then reduce inequalities in incomes by constantly maintaining and bringing up to date our system of progressive taxation. We must do it by the provision of social services which are available to all, regardless of income; for a man who suddenly has new medical services available to him and his family, or a new house, or a new school or community centre, has had an improvement in his standard of living, just as much as if he had more money in his pocket. And we must also concentrate the wage incomes which increased productivity makes possible on to the lowest paid workers in our society.

But it would be quite wrong for us to aim at complete equality of income between all workers. Incomes must depend upon work and output too; there must be an incentive for everyone to work a little harder. The central point about our wages policy must be that, while it prevents gross inequalities, it creates a direct link between productivity and income. Wherever appropriate piece-rates should be employed, or bonuses paid for increased output. And where this is not possible—for example, in jobs like teaching or nursing—we should take account of the social usefulness of the work, and its relative attractiveness in comparison with other opportunities for earning a living—including farming.

This means that there is an important constructive task for NUTA and for TANU. We must recognize that the way to increase our members' standard of living is by helping them to become more productive at whatever job they are doing. Our trade union movement must shake off its British heritage, where it found its justification for existence by quarrelling with the employers. The largest employer in Tanzania now is the people—their Government and their public institutions. NUTA must learn something from the Soviet trade unions, or the Swedish ones. Both of these, in their different ways, are chiefly concerned with ensuring that the wage-earners get a fair share of an increased value of output. Thus they first work to encourage and to help improve productivity, and then argue about its fair distribution. This is, of course, a more difficult task than just making demands for wage increases. But it is a task which is a real service to the members of the trade union movement and to the people as a whole. Nor should this task be left only to NUTA. TANU leaders also have a responsibility, for wage-earners as well as peasants are members of our political movement.

## Rural Development

I have spent a long time on this matter because it is important that we should all understand these basic economic facts of Tanzania. We are now a poor nation; there is no short cut to prosperity; hard work and a deliberate decision by us to plan for a better future is the only way forward. Once we accept these things then we can work and plan to make sure that our progress takes us in the right direction. We can then ensure that increasing prosperity is used for the benefit of the people as a whole and not concentrated in the hands of a few. We can ensure that we build a society in which men co-operate together for their mutual benefit. And we can nurture the traditional values of Africa—the belief that man as a member of his community must enjoy respect and well-being alongside his fellows, and in proportion to his contribution to the society of which he is a member.

For the vast majority of our people the community will continue to be a rural one, and the means of livelihood will be agriculture. This means that our agriculture must be organized in such a manner that improved conditions become possible for all who are willing to work, and that our rural life must be based on the principles of socialism—that is, on the principles of equality, co-operation, and democracy.

In traditional African life the people were equal, they co-operated together, and they participated in all the decisions which affected their lives. But the equality was an equality of poverty; the co-operation was on small things; and their government was only the government of their own family unit, and of their clan, or at most of their tribe. Our task, therefore, is to modernize the traditional structure so as to make it meet our new aspirations for a higher standard of living.

This can be done provided we hold fast to the basic principles of traditional living, while we adapt its techniques to those of the twentieth century. And the way to do this is to create all over Tanzania economic and social communities where people live together and work together for the good of all, and which are inter-locked so that all of the different communities also work together in co-operation for the common good of the nation as a whole.

This is the objective outlined in the policy paper 'Socialism and Rural Development' to which I wish to direct the attention of this Conference. This paper is the application of the Arusha Declaration to the practical needs of our rural life. It is vital that it be clearly understood, and that we should all work for its implementation. For 'Socialism and Rural Development' is an outline of socialism and self-reliance as it applies to Tanzania's rural life and rural people; and that means as it applies to 95 per cent of our population.

In our countryside there will be national projects; state farms, state forests, national parks, and so on. But these will not be the dominating type of organization for the rural areas. They will be created and run to cater for special problems and special needs. The way the majority of our people will live and work in a socialist Tanzania will be in villages which they themselves create and govern, and which are the basis for the productive activities of the members.

Let us put this objective in its simplest terms. A group of families will live together in a village, and will work together on a common farm for their common benefit. Their houses will be the ones they build for themselves out of their own resources; their farm will be owned jointly, and its produce will be their joint property. The activities of the village, and the type of production they undertake, as well as the distribution of crops and other goods they produce, will all be determined by the village members themselves. For the land will be 'our land' to all the members of the village; the crops will be 'our crops'; the common herd of animals will be 'our herd'. In other words, we shall have an up-to-date, and larger, version of the traditional African family, where the land was 'ours', crops were 'ours', and so on.

The size and composition of the group of people who live together will vary from one part of the country to another, depending upon the soil, the appropriate crops or animal husbandry, and the social customs of the people. But by living together and working together, all of them will be able to be better off. Instead of 40 different families each living separately and each farming their own land, collecting their own water, and sending their children miles to school, they will come together and live in a village. Then, by their joint efforts, they will—in time—be able to bring water into the village; they will be able to build their children's school conveniently near all of them; they will be able to build a community centre and a store for their mutual convenience, and so on. Also, by working together on one farm they will soon be able to invest in an oxen-plough to do much of the work each had previously to do with his own hoe and panga; they will be able to take full advantage of skilled advice about modern methods; they will be able to increase their joint production and their joint prosperity. They will be able jointly to arrange the sale of their produce, and the purchase of the goods they want to buy from outside —perhaps by running their own ujamaa shop. And so on. In other words, a living and working community will have been created. All members of the community will be equal in status and any variations of income will reflect only differences in the amount of work done. They will be working in co-operation, and not in opposition to each other; and they will be governing their own village affairs as well as being able to discuss together national issues which affect them as citizens of Tanzania.

This is the objective. It is stated clearly, and at greater length, in the policy paper. We must understand it so that we know what we are working towards. But it is not something we shall achieve overnight. We have a long way to go.

For what has been happening over recent years is quite different. We have not been enlarging and modernizing our traditional family unit as much as abandoning it in favour of small-scale capitalist farming. Many of our most dynamic and energetic farmers, especially those with the most initiative and willingness to learn new techniques, have been branching out on their own as individuals. They have not been enlarging their farms by joining with others in a spirit of equality, but by employing labour. So we are getting the beginnings of the development of an agricultural labouring class on the one hand, and a wealthier employing class on the other. Fortunately, this development has not gone very far; we can arrest the trend without difficulty. But we must not make this change by persecuting the progressive farmers; after all, we have been encouraging them in the direction they have been going! Instead we must seek their co-operation, and integrate them into the new socialist agriculture by showing them that their best interests will be served by this development. For energy and initiative such as these farmers have displayed will be very important to our progress. We need these people.

How then do we move from our present system to the system of ujamaa villages? The policy paper outlines some of the steps which may be used in different places, but it is important to remember two things. First, that the appropriate first steps will be different in different places. And second, that the people themselves must decide whether and when they are prepared to make this movement. For we are not simply trying to organize increased production; we are trying to introduce a whole new way of life for the majority of our people. This can only be done once the people understand its purposes and voluntarily decide to participate.

We must not try to rush this development; what matters is not the speed but the direction in which we move. We must encourage and help people, not try to force them. For this kind of village does exist in Tanzania, and the members of them are learning their advantages. But sometimes people have tried to start this kind of thing and have failed. The reason is often that their expectations were too great; they had too much enthusiasm and too much impatience. What is needed is careful thought and planning —by the people themselves. This is why it is better to start slowly, perhaps by working a common plot in addition to private ones, perhaps by undertaking 'mutual help'. Then as the problems reveal themselves, and are solved by the participants, so they will gain confidence and take the next step.

But 'slowly' does not mean 'without determination'. The initiative for movements in the direction of ujamaa villages can be taken by anyone who understands the objective. It does not have to be a TANU leader, or Government official. Anyone can get together with a group of friends and decide to start. For these villages must govern them-selves; the participants must control their own activities. No one else can do it for them. Thus a group of young people may decide to start; or the members of a TANU cell; or the members of a church or a mosque. Or the school teacher in a village school can take the initiative by asking the children's parents to work with the school in a common project—and so on.

The job of TANU leaders is to help, and to encourage. This will not always be easy. Sometimes people will be sceptical or they will reject the advice and make mistakes. But if the TANU leaders are themselves participants in such schemes, and are able to demonstrate by example the benefits of, and the best methods for, this kind of activity, then success will be greater. We have to act ourselves, and then others will follow. If every MP or other delegate here from a rural area decides to be a member of an ujamaa village, we shall make a good start. Indeed, no one who can live in an ujamaa village, but does not, should talk about ujamaa!

One other important point for TANU leaders to remember is that there can be no great promises of Government help, nor of immediate prosperity, if such villages are started. It is safer to assume that the Government will be able to give no help at all than to assume that Government will come in with all the advice or capital which could possibly be required! And the truth is that at the beginning life in an ujamaa village will be just as hard as the life of a farmer working on his own. This system is no substitute for hard work. It just means that the hard work will, in time, bring greater returns.

For an ujamaa village, as outlined in this paper, is both a socialist, and a self-reliant, community. It will be using local resources and traditional knowledge, and working up from these to the simple improvements which are possible when people work together. As the villages succeed, the members will graduate from hoes to ox-ploughs, from carrying everything on their heads to using bicycles, or ox-carts. They will work out their own system of social security and assistance in time of trouble. They will be self-reliant ujamaa communities. When the Government and other national institutions come in, they will do so to supplement the activities of the members and assist them to help themselves.

If we succeed in starting ujamaa villages, we shall be able to build up from them to village associations, whereby a number of villages work together for purposes which are too big for any of them separately. And we shall later be able to develop rural industries to diversify and improve life in the rural areas. But all these things depend upon our moving in the right direction, and starting at the bottom with the people coming together in a spirit of equality to work for their common betterment.

*Conclusion*

This Conference has a great deal of serious business before it. But one of the most important things is a consideration of 'Socialism and Rural Development'. This paper should be regarded as an integral part of the Arusha Declaration, and we should therefore give it a great deal of attention here. We have already taken many decisions about the industrial and commercial sector of our economy; we have taken decisions about the responsibilities and qualifications of leadership. Now is the time for us to think deeply and seriously about the way forward for the masses of our people, and therefore for us all.

I believe that by accepting this paper, and by returning home with a determination to work for its implementation, we shall be setting a pattern which will be our pride and our satisfaction in the years to come.

# 9

# Progress in the Rural Areas

*A speech to the University College branch of TANU Youth League to open a seminar on the policy booklet 'Socialism and Rural Development', 21 January 1968.*

I am extremely pleased that the University Branch of the TANU Youth League has selected the policy paper 'Socialism and Rural Development' for serious study. For in some ways this policy is a problem; it is very difficult to get it organized and implemented. The new education policy outlined in 'Education for Self-Reliance' can be—and is being—worked out in some detail by the Ministry of Education; they can organize its introduction, and supervise the action being taken on it. Of course, a very great deal still depends upon the teachers and principals in schools throughout the country—upon their initiative and understanding. But in this field you do have a recognizable group, all of whom are public employees, to whom the new policy can be explained; you can direct your guidance and assistance easily to the right places, and you can supervise developments almost as they occur.

The policy paper we are talking about today is very different. It is directed at all the people of Tanzania—or at least all of those who live in the rural areas. It is an outline of a policy of inter-linked self-governing village communities which are of the people, and which therefore cannot be created for them or imposed on them. The paper therefore calls for leadership, but not for orders to be given; it directs the people along the socialist path, but excludes any attempt to whip them into it—saying clearly that you cannot force people to lead socialist lives.

This inevitably creates a difficulty, for it leaves open the question of how the Government can actively promote ujamaa villages on a healthy basis. Indeed, there are two opposing dangers at the outset; on the one hand there is a danger that enthusiastic TANU members and others might rush out and bully people into artificial communities which will collapse with the first breath of adversity, and on the other there is a danger that nothing will happen at all. It is a little early to say which of these traps we are falling into—after all, the paper was only published in September and it would certainly take longer than three months for a soundly based community of this kind to get beyond the talking stage.

In opening this Seminar today, however, I do not intend to justify the principles laid down in 'Socialism and Rural Development', nor to describe its proposals. I am assuming that you have read and studied the document, so that what you require from me is two things; the raising of problems, and the answering of any points which are unclear!

The first problem which must be faced is the one I have already referred to: how do we get started? The policy is there, with the goals clearly stated. The document suggests that any Tanzanian can take the initiative. Fine! But how do we move from the fact that any Tanzanian may and can take the initiative to the fact of his doing so?

In considering this question it is absolutely essential that the crucial point about an ujamaa village-farm should not be forgotten. The community must own, control, and run its own activities. They must be democratic and socialist, working and living communities, in which the members are jointly responsible to themselves. Does this mean that

they must therefore be started by the members without
outside initiative or participation? In considering this
question we have to remember that the vast majority of our
people are still illiterate; they could not read and study
this policy document even if it were easily available to
them. The people in our rural areas will have heard about
ujamaa villages on the radio, or through talk—if they have
heard of them at all!

How then do we get moving? Government and TANU
leaders could certainly encourage, explain and teach about
these ideas; but is this enough? Would it really help very
much if every person in this Seminar simply talked about
the policy in his home area during the vacation, and then
came back to the towns? What of the idea that more
educated people should join the practical work of initiating
an ujamaa village, and become a founder member of it?
Is it likely that we should have any volunteers for such
work when it is realized how hard, and how materially
unrewarding, it will be in comparison with the opportunities open to educated people—even after Arusha?

I am putting these questions frankly, because I think
they must be answered. The fact that I pose them should
not be taken to imply that I think there is no answer, or
that it is necessarily a discouraging one! My own experience suggests that our people in the rural areas are
prepared to work together for their common good; in
many places they have never stopped this traditional
custom, and would take quite easily to an extension of it.
The problem is not the principle; the problem is that of
getting people to adopt practices which retain the central
idea at the same time as they allow for development and
growth. For we are not just trying to go backwards into
the traditional past; we are trying to retain the traditional
values of human equality and dignity while taking advantage

of modern knowledge about the advantages of scale and improved tools. But inevitably this requires some adaptation in traditional social organization; it requires a conscious working together for the common good, and a conscious effort to utilize the strength of united activity for social purposes. In the past we worked together because that was the custom; now we have to do it deliberately and to do it in such a manner that modern knowledge can be utilized for the common good.

One thing is certainly known; nothing succeeds like success! If we can get a few of these village communities working in every area, their success will lead to others also being started. The essential thing therefore is to begin. It is for this reason that the paper suggests that anyone can take the initiative, and suggests also that a small handful of people—the members of a ten-house cell or an even smaller number—could begin. Of course, such a small unit would not be able to achieve very much; but it can grow. The present 12 ujamaa villages in the Ruvuma Development Association have grown out of a beginning made by 10 individuals, and the fact that after a complete crop failure in the first year, 3 of those 10 were prepared to try again the following year.

There is in fact an advantage in starting very small, in that the members will know each other well and be able to work together to overcome the inevitable difficulties without taking refuge in blaming others. Because there are only a few of them they will be able to discuss their problems together, and make decisions together for which they all feel equally responsible. Yet there obviously comes a point below which you cannot fall and still have an ujamaa village. What is the ideal size? Will it vary very much in different conditions? And how can you determine what the optimum figure is and reach it?

In all this discussion we must realize the central fact:
that an ujamaa village must be governed by the members
themselves, equally. I have already stated this once this
morning, but I make no apology for saying it again;
it is the essence of rural socialism. Members must jointly
make their own decisions on everything which is of ex-
clusive concern to the village—where to plant, what to
plant, how to share the work, how to share the returns,
what to invest in the future development, and so on.
Obviously the communities, and their members, must obey
the laws of the land; they cannot be exempt from taxation
or other national responsibilities. But the decisions about
the way they run their farm and their village—the amount of
private farming and ownership they allow etc.—must be
made by them, not by others.

There will, in fact, probably be no shortage of people who
come to a new embryonic village and tell the members what
to do. Indeed, I hope the agricultural field workers and
other skilled and trained people will be offering their
advice freely, and doing all they can to encourage ujamaa
villages to adopt modern methods from the start. But the
decisions must be made by the members, not by anyone
else—even Area Commissioners or visiting Presidents!

Yet we must be clear what we are saying here. For we
have a real dilemma; it may easily happen that a visiting
political or Government leader knows that the people are
making a mistake which could prove fatal to their ambition,
either in organization, in their selection of their leader,
or in their methods. The temptation to intervene must
surely be very great indeed under these circumstances;
part of the visitor's job is to help these communities.
Obviously he should explain his point, illustrate his argument by pointing to experience elsewhere, and discuss
the whole question with the members. But suppose the

members still insist on their own decision? It is at that point that we have to go back to the essence of these villages; people must be allowed to make their own decisions, and therefore their own mistakes. Only if we accept this are we really accepting the philosophy of socialism and rural development. If we prevent people making their own mistakes we are preventing the establishment of ujamaa villages; we can advise and warn, but if we try to run them we are destroying them. We may have to pay a price in failures and disappointments as a result, but it cannot be avoided. And in any case obstinate local people can sometimes prove all previous experience, and all skilled advice to be wrong! The fact that a man is employed by Government, or elected in TANU—or even educated at the University College—does not make him infallible!

In one sense all that I have been saying so far is a call for leadership. We need people to lead others into an understanding of the concept of ujamaa villages, to lead the members in the villages, to promote good methods of husbandry and practical methods of organization; we need people to rally the members when they get discouraged, show them the way out of their difficulties, and so on. Progress in socialist rural development does in fact depend almost entirely on leadership at all levels; it needs leadership to get the groups started, and it needs leadership to maintain them and have them grow.

Let me emphasize that this leadership I am now talking about does not imply control any more than it implies bullying or intimidating people. A good leader will explain, teach and inspire. In an ujamaa village he will do more. He will lead by doing. He is in the front of the people, showing them what can be done, guiding them, and encouraging them. But he is with them. You do not lead people by being so far in front, or so theoretical in your teaching that the people cannot see what you are doing or saying. You do not lead people by yapping at their heels like a dog herding cattle. You can lead the people only by being one of them, but just being more active as well as more thoughtful, and more willing to teach as well as more willing to learn—from them and others.

The members of an ujamaa village must control their own affairs—I say it again! But the role of a leader is crucial, and good leadership will make all the difference to the socialist success and the material success of such a community.

Let me give one example of the kind of leadership which is needed. Suppose a group of families have decided to start a co-operative farm and village, and are discussing where to build their houses. The problem is whether to build on a hill or down in the valley; and the argument is about the ease of getting water versus the danger of flooding. A good leader who is a member of this group may argue that it is better to build on the hill and face the drudgery of carrying the water until they can afford a pump and pipes; but let us suppose that despite all his efforts the general opinion is to build near the water's edge. What should he do? The answer is clear: he must play a very full part in the work of building the village in the valley. Having done that he must also think out plans for action if his fears are proved well-founded. He might persuade the members to build some of their stores on the hill so as to have a reserve in case of trouble; he might persuade them to keep on the hill a reserve of poles and thatching material which can then be used wherever and whenever it is necessary; and he will certainly work out in his own mind a plan for rescue and shelter on higher ground so that he at least knows what must be done in case of emergency.

But this kind of leadership is only one of many different kinds which will be needed. There is the same problem of management—although on a different scale—for an ujamaa farm as for a capitalist farm which employs many people. Work has still to be organized, the crops harvested and sold, etc. This will require some delegation, by the members, of the power over themselves—for you cannot have a members' meeting every day in order to decide whether to weed the beans or the tobacco! The selection of the right person as the 'farm manager' or as the 'farm treasurer' can be of vital importance. How then can the members be helped to choose the best man from among their number? And if they do make a mistake, how can they be sure of effecting a change without having so much daily 'democracy' in the running of the farm that no work gets done because of the time spent in talking?

These are practical questions. The little experience we have so far in Tanzania shows the importance of the village leaders. It is clear they must be strong men, yet humble; they must be capable of ensuring that everyone does a fair share of the work—including themselves—and at the same time they must be willing to accept group decisions on basic issues. For example, they must be able to convince the members that everyone will have to work for eight hours a day in order to get through all the jobs; able to accept a group decision that this will be done from 6.00 a.m. until 2.00 p.m.; and then able to allocate different members to different jobs in rotation—and see that they are done!

This brings me to the final problem which I intend to refer to today—the problem of incentives. For it is all very well to say that members will 'live together and work together for the common good'; it is all very well to say a leader's job is to see that everyone does his fair share. But we are not all angels, and it is not unknown for everyone to do a fair share on a communal project just because

everyone does as much as the laziest member, and no more!
What kind of organization, or what kind of rules about
distribution of returns, should be recommended to groups
setting up together, so as to ensure that between them
they produce the maximum? For if there is no difference
in return, is it not likely that the good and fast worker may
get tired of putting his best efforts forward while another
member merely does the bare minimum which keeps him
in the scheme? In an ideal world he might shrug his shoul-
ders and carry on; in the world as it is he might decide to
do less himself too!

Is it enough therefore, to rely upon every member
understanding the benefit to himself of everyone putting
forward his maximum effort? Is it enough to rely upon
social sanctions as a discipline against those who slack,
with expulsion as the only and final weapon against them?
Or would such groups be advised to work out some system
of division according to the amount of work done, or the
number of hours spent on the communal projects? If you
do this, are you breaking the socialist principle of equality—
for it will lead to some differences in income between the
members? And if you do not do it, are you allowing the
poor workers, or the lazy ones, to exploit the others? But
again, if you do advocate payment by work done, what
about those people who work to the best of their ability,
but who are sick, or weak, or just not very capable?

Mr. Chairman, there are many other problems I could
raise—some of which may be raised by other speakers.
For the policy outlined in 'Socialism and Rural Development' is not the work of a month or a year; it is the work
for ten or twenty years ahead. What we have to do now is
start; and the more people who understand the objectives,
and who are willing to join in, the greater—and the quicker
—will be our success.